WITHDRAWN

— by —
Winnetka Public Library

'93

# Angelic Healing

ALSO BY EILEEN ELIAS FREEMAN

*Touched by Angels*

*The Angels' Little Instruction Book*

# Angelic Healing

## Working with Your Angels to Heal Your Life

### Eileen Elias Freeman

WARNER BOOKS

A Time Warner Company

*To Enniss,*
*my dear friend and companion,*
*who leads me patiently*
*to God*
*and*
*to Raphael,*
*his chief, archangel and*
*throne of God, whose*
*healing counsels have helped me*
*immeasurably in living—and writing—*
*this book*

Copyright © 1994 by Eileen Freeman
All rights reserved.

Warner Books, Inc., 1271 Avenue of the Americas, New York, NY 10020

**W** A Time Warner Company

Printed in the United States of America
First Printing: November 1994
10 9 8 7 6 5 4 3 2 1

**Library of Congress Cataloging-in-Publication Data**

Freeman, Eileen E.
    Angelic healing : working with your angels to heal your life/
Eileen Elias Freeman.
        p.    cm.
    Includes bibliographical references.
    ISBN 0-446-51846-8
    1. Angels.    2. Healing—Religious aspects.    I. Title.
BL477.F73    1994
291.2'15—dc20                                                                94-9583
                                                                                   CIP

*Book design by Giorgetta Bell McRee*
*Endpaper art from* Spiritual Beginning, *a painting by Andy Lakey*

"Honor physicians for their services, for the Lord created them, and their gift of healing comes from the Most High.

"The Lord created medicines from the earth, and the sensible person will not despise them. By them physicians heal and take away pain, and through them healing spreads over all the earth.

"My child, when you are ill, do not delay, but pray to the Lord to be healed.

"Give up your faults and direct your hands rightly, and cleanse your heart from all evil.

"Offer a sweet-smelling sacrifice, and pour oil on your offering, then give the physicians their place, for the Lord has created them.

"Do not let them leave you, for you need them. There may come a time when recovery lies in the hands of physicians, for they, too, pray to the Lord to grant them success in diagnosis and in healing, for the preservation of life."

—Sirach 38:1–14

*I call this the Angelic Heart™. It is the symbol I use for
everything. The wings remind us that our hearts were
meant to fly with the angels. The halo tells us we are
surrounded by healing light at all times. Most important,
the heart is always open, because if you close your
heart, you can neither let love in nor give it to others.
Angels' hearts are always open.
May yours be open, too.*

# Contents

## Contents

# Contents

# Foreword

"*If we are not committed to seeking God, we will never be able to establish a fruitful relationship with our angels.*"

When I wrote *Touched by Angels* in 1992, I said that, in my opinion, those were the most important words in the book. Now that I have come to write a second book on angels, I reiterate that belief.

*Touched by Angels* dealt with the way friendships with our special angel often begin and how they touch—and change—our lives. I gave some striking examples of how a variety of people—men, women, children, from all backgrounds and walks of life—had been befriended by their angels, and how their lives had grown from their angels' touch.

Angels want to be our friends. They are companions on the journey of life on this planet, ancient fellow travelers, whose love and light and wisdom can enrich our lives immeasurably. They want to share with us and help us grow toward the unique spiritual destiny that is ours. Their guidance and support is wonderful, something to rejoice in and to give thanks for.

And the thanks go—primarily, and in the first place—to the Source from whom both we and the angels come. The angels themselves are not that Source. They are not divine, although they, like ourselves, are immortals. If their faces shine with unearthly light, it is because they are filled with the one Light. Nothing in them darkens that light; they are magnifying glasses that catch a fraction of the glory and concentrate it for us so we can see it, even as they do.

Angels, as I have said, are our friends, not our tools. We cannot use them as we do a can opener, to get at the stuff inside. They know all of our little tricks and avoid such attempts easily and consistently. Sometimes I think that the greatest sin in our self-centered world is the way we use people and things to get our way.

Nor are angels our personal servants, to whom we can give orders. They serve God, who is Love, and the only agenda they know is the divine plan.

Unfortunately, it seems that whenever something truly wonderful comes to light—like the work of the angels in our lives—there are those who try to trade on it. They may say they can promise a quick fix, instant enlightenment. In the wake of people's interest in angels and hunger for more information about them and how to be in touch with them, we are now seeing some goods and "services" being offered that go beyond mere foolishness and wind up in the realm of pure quackery—or worse.

Some of these companies will guarantee to communicate with your angel for you. Some will sell you objects they claim will do the same thing. And of course, they want significant amounts of money for such things. And as if that weren't enough, some less than reliable publications have started printing stories about angels that can hardly be worthy of credibility.

It's important for those who are interested in the angels not to be suckered by such specious promises and improbable stories. It's essential to test any such promises and offers against what we know to be true about angelic natures and purposes.

For example, I recently received a booklet from something calling itself the California Astrology Association, with a flyer about angels. According to the flyer, we can talk to our angels until we're blue in the face, but they won't listen unless we address our prayers directly to "an authentic image" of our angel, in which case we can command them to do virtually anything for us, including winning the lottery, finding a perfect mate, etc. Coincidentally, the association was offering just such an "authentic" image: a cheap medallion at a not-so-cheap price.

I also had an offer from a numerologist, who said she specialized in angels. Normally her readings cost $250, but for a limited time they were just $125—and if I recommended others to her services, she would give me $25 for each reading she did. She also said I was an angel on the same level as Vice President Gore and that President Clinton could also aspire to being an angel. Just for the record, I'm not.

A group called the Collectors Library in Illinois also offered something called *The Angel Collectors Handbook* and sent out advertisements early in 1993 to members of the two national collectors' clubs. To date, no one I know ever had their orders filled.

Another individual has been sending out personalized packets offering a Supernatural 240 Hour Window and voluntering to send buyers a cosmic-ray repair kit, which she states is the reason why most people can't see and hear their angels. Once they receive this kit, they will learn how "to clear the obstructions in their cosmic current," which will enable gifts of their own choosing to flow into their spiritual bank account.

And various mediums "guarantee" to contact angels for other people, usually for a heavy fee.

All of these are trading on our innate, intense longing for God and our ultimate destiny as children of God to become perfected, filled with love and light and joy, so that in the next dimension we will see God face-to-face, as it were, and continue to grow and evolve beyond anything we can imagine here on earth. And given the nature of American society, the desire for a "quick fix" is all too prevalent. Some people figure, "If I can get instant enlightenment through someone else, why should I bother taking the time to meditate, to pray, to try to get the darkness out of my life and live in love and in service to others? I'll just buy my enlightenment." I assure you, it won't work.

And as if angelic hucksters aren't enough, a supermarket tabloid has recently run articles in which a nurse purportedly took the first-ever photo of an angel appearing on a hospital lawn to cure children of cancer, and NASA taped angelic music in outer space. Another one said that actor Michael Landon, who had played the role of an angel in *Highway to Heaven,* and who had just died of cancer, had just been assigned to earth—as an angel!

The story reminds me of one I saw in another tabloid a year or so ago. It showed a picture of a baby supposedly born with angel wings—*My little angel! gushed the mother of the child.* According to the article, the baby was now nine months old, and the wings were starting to move on their own. *Who knows how long before he actually starts flying?*

I strongly urge you not to be taken in by such things. Remember that angels are always with us, but that they only manifest themselves to us when God wills. We can't force it, nor should we try. The more we live our lives for God, in love and joy, in light and peace, and in service to others, the closer our angels will be to us and the more we will sense their presence and loving help to enable us to heal our lives.

And that's the truth.

—Eileen Elias Freeman
*December 1993*

# Acknowledgments

*Acknowledgment* still seems as inadequate a word as it did when I wrote *Touched by Angels*. If I could retitle the head on this page, I would say instead, "Immense, Overwhelming Love and Gratitude." But I think my copy editor might take issue with the form, if not with the content, so I'll be conventional (this time).

My heartfelt gratitude goes to:

## On The Divine Side

To Jesus, whom alone I worship as God, who has saved me from the darkness and showed me the incredible destiny of the sons and daughters of God: "In the sight of the angels may I sing your praise!"

# On The Angelic Side

Naturally, first thanks go to Enniss, my beloved guardian angel and friend, whose guidance has been at times gentle and forceful, serious and funny. I love you.

To Raphael, Enniss's chief in the order of guardians, who is set over the healing of the earth and the souls of all who dwell on it—I bless God for your inspiration and your help as I wrote this book, and I pray that all those who read it will call upon God to send you into every corner of our planet to bring the divine light and healing that we all need.

To Tallithia, my recording angel, who helped me to remember more about healing in my life than I ever thought I could—thank you for your patience, dear heart.

To Kennisha, my angelic defender, whose light scatters the darkness—may my thanks resound from one end of heaven to the other.

# On The Human Side

To Jana and Michael and John and "Pak" and "Annaliese," who were so kind as to let me use their stories of healing for this book, who gave of themselves until we all cried in wonder at the love of God.

To John Ronner, author of *Do You Have a Guardian Angel?* and *Know Your Angels*, whose friendship, support, and practical wisdom have been an immense blessing in my life.

To Bruce Lancaster and all the reference staff of Drew University's Rose Memorial Library, for going out of their way time and time again to help me find the materials I needed—and I wasn't even a student.

To Andy Lakey, my dear friend, whose angel art enhances the endpapers of both this book and *Touched by Angels*. His art enables me to feel the inherent power and energy of the angels, their single-mindedness and devotion, without mixing up irrelevant concepts like sex, race, age, culture, and all those other human characteristics that we must get past in order to appreciate other representations of angels.

To the hundreds of people who wrote to me after *Touched by Angels* was published, to share their love, their wisdom, and their own stories of angelic love and healing. Thank you from the depths of my heart for your letters. They have filled me with joy and fueled my prayers of thanks ever since you began writing.

To all the beautiful people in the AngelWatch Network, whose thoughtful prayers and phone calls enabled me to finish this book, especially Darlene McCullough, whose gift of vitamins gave me a lot more than just energy of body, and Dolores Devine, whose loving concern was healing in a special way.

I wish you all peace and joy in your search for God and the angels.

# Chapter One
# Angelic Healing

*Then an angel from heaven appeared to him, strengthening him.*

—Luke 22:43

ou have cancer, Ms. Freeman, a very serious cancer," the doctor sadly said to me. "We won't have the lab tests from your D and C back officially until tomorrow, but I want you to be prepared. I've been a gynecological surgeon for thirty years, and all the signs are unmistakable. Your uterus is clearly involved, probably your cervix, too, and it is quite possible that the cancer may have already spread through the wall of the uterus into the abdominal cavity. We won't know just how bad it is until we do the surgery. I'm so sorry."

Anyone who has ever heard the scary words, "You have cancer," knows how I felt in that moment back in 1986 when the doctor sat beside my hospital bed to give me the fateful news. To say I was devastated would be

1

an understatement of vast proportions. I had just received a promotion at the educational company I worked for, my life was moving at a happy pace, I was writing and speaking more about angels, and I was the sole support of my mother, who had been widowed five years before. It was not the time for radical changes, or so I thought.

My world crashed in around me. I was screaming for help, crying out in disbelief. *This can't be happening to me*, I protested, looking around as if I'd find the person the doctor was *really* talking to.

In about three seconds, ten pages of thoughts went through my head, all of them dire and full of fear and gloom: *What will happen to Mother if I die? How long do I have to live? Do I need to make a will, or . . .*

I'm not accustomed to living in fear, as those who have read my first book, *Touched by Angels*, know. In it I described my encounter as a child of five with my guardian angel, who came to comfort me after the death of my grandmother, and to take away the many fears that were strangling my young life. After the angel left, I realized that I was no longer afraid of anything, least of all dying.

But now, as I sat up in bed crying, and feeling cold, I *was* afraid. Terror of an unknown future or lack thereof rolled over me like an avalanche and buried me under tons of ice. *You're gonna die, you're gonna die*, a horrible, mocking voice screamed in my ear. At that moment, it was the only voice I could hear, and it drowned out everything else. I felt as though I would explode. I passed out, briefly.

The next thing I remember is feeling a prick on my arm. I turned to look and saw a nurse with a hypodermic in her hand.

"What was that?" I asked, my voice brittle with tension.

"Just a little something to help reduce your blood pressure," she replied. "It spiked while the doctor was speaking with you. Just lie back, please; you'll probably feel a little light-headed."

For an instant I had forgotten about the doctor and his gloomy message. Cancer. Cancer. Cancer. The word kept burning in my brain, and the medication did nothing to stop the searing pain in my soul. All it did was make me so limp physically that only my brain would work. It didn't even stop the adrenaline pumping through my system. It was as if the cancer in my body was a saber-toothed tiger and I was a lone cavewoman trying to outrun it, forced to race along the circular pathways of my veins and arteries with no way out.

I lay there, cold and terrified. The cold was more than physical; it was preternatural. I remembered afterwards that it was just like the cold that had surrounded me the night Enniss came to reassure me. I had been sitting up in bed, then, too, feeling as if I were inside a walk-in freezer or a meat processing plant, rank with the smell of bloody ice and rancid food. Even the air was frosty.

At that point, the nasty little voices came back in greater strength, with their message of fear and anxiety. Coldly rational (and all the more terrifying for that) fantasies of the future crowded in on me again.

And then I heard that still, small voice in my heart that I had long since come to know as Enniss's voice, my guardian angel, who, by the grace of God, watches over me and has since I was conceived. And it said, *Don't be afraid, Eileen. There is nothing to be afraid of.*

These were the same words I had heard in my childhood when I first saw Enniss. They were the first positive words I had heard since the doctor's pronouncement of doom, and I clung to them as a drowning woman would cling to a life preserver. They broke the domination of the voices of fear that were deafening me, and I was able to talk to the One I needed to touch.

"O dear God, please help me!" I cried aloud, tears pouring from my eyes. "I don't know what to do."

I will always be grateful to Enniss for repeating those words from my childhood at that moment, for they broke into the conversation I was being forced into with the spirits of fear, and gave me room to do what I most needed to do: to pray, to touch God and let myself be touched in return, to restore the natural balance. Until Enniss broke in (and it seemed to me that he did most forcefully interrupt), the spirits of fear were so overwhelming that I couldn't even reach out to God.

In fact, until I heard Enniss's loving and wise words, and until I turned my heart outward to God, I couldn't even recognize these terrible voices for what they were: the malice of those fallen angels who try, out of hate and envy, to ruin our lives with fear. They had chosen the moment when I first learned I had cancer to dump on me all the fear they could, hoping to turn my heart from God.

Enniss, of course, was more than a match for them; all the servants of God are. His subtlety in reminding me of God's word to me, a word I have always found to be true, was what I needed at that moment. I was able to realize that the voices were not coming from inside me, a reflection of some deep-seated fear in my soul. Rather, they were voices from without, the whisperings of other beings, evil, envious, discontented, unutterably sad.

4

The moment enlightenment hit, and I understood that the voices were those of the fallen angels, I was healed of the spiritual paralysis that had taken me over. I was able to deal with the voices of doom. I spoke to them out of my faith, reminding them that I am the daughter of God and telling them that I was on to them and would no longer listen to anything they had to say. I was angry that they had invaded the outskirts of my consciousness at a time when I was so vulnerable, and I said so.

"You poor sad creatures," I added. (Nothing unnerves them more than to be pitied by a human being.) "Don't you have anything more positive to do than pester me? Get a life! And leave mine alone."

Coming as I do out of a Christian faith, I told them that my trust was in Jesus, my Savior, and unless they wanted to have an uplifting conversation with me about *Him*, we had nothing to say to each other and they could just leave me alone.

They left me alone.

Once I was finally free of the voices, the mindless terror left, too, and the only fear that remained in me began to dissipate as the extra adrenaline in my system was dissolved. The foul, cold atmosphere also faded, and the room returned to normal.

I heaved a small sigh of relief. "Dear God, thank you for sending Enniss to remind me that I never need to be afraid," I prayed gratefully.

"Enniss, my faithful angel, thank you for being so good at your job," I added.

*My pleasure, dear heart; you know it is my joy to serve.*

Reassured a little, I sat up in bed and began to take stock of my situation. Even without the voices clamoring in my ear, it was still scary to think that deep down inside me, rogue cells were busy multiplying and dividing and taking over normal cells with abandon. I didn't feel any different.

Of course I should have noticed the warning signs I had been having for several months, but I always had severe PMS, not to mention MS and even PostMS (if there are such things). I didn't really think it could happen to me.

"Why didn't you warn me, Enniss?" I asked a bit reproachfully.

*I did, child. You wouldn't pay attention,* he answered. *But here you are, after all. Isn't that what's important?*

"Sorry, you're right as usual," I apologized.

I tried to think calmly about what to do, deciding I wouldn't tell my mother until the lab tests were back. She had a serious heart condition, and I was concerned about what the news that her only child had cancer might do to her.

Then it hit me: the doctor hadn't known for *sure* I had cancer; he only said that in his professional opinion it *looked* like a cancer.

I heaved a sigh of relief. Of course he is wrong, I thought. It's not cancer, just some other serious problem. They can probably treat it with medication. Let's not borrow troubles. In fact, why not just ask for a miracle? Surely God would send Enniss to do that for me.

So I asked God for a miracle. With as much humility and fervor as I could muster, I asked Him to cure whatever it was I had so that I could go on living my life as I had been. "Think of my mother," I asked God. "You wouldn't want to leave her alone if anything happened to me. What would she do?"

I went on and on, dredging up every reason I could think of why God should do a miracle in my life and heal my body of whatever it was that had made me ill.

"When they do the tests, let them turn out negative," I pleaded. "Please, dear God, answer my prayer."

And God did indeed answer my prayer. The answer was *No*, a loving no, but no nonetheless.

The tests came back positive—in spades.

I remember the moment when I got the call. I had been discharged from the hospital, and so sure was I that everything would be all right, I had gone to a science fiction convention I had been planning to attend. I was in my hotel room changing for the costume parade when the phone rang.

"Eileen . . ." My mother's quavering voice told me all I needed to know without another word. My heart sank.

"Oh, dear God!" I replied. My knees were weak, and I sat heavily on the bed. All thoughts of being the best-dressed "Time Lord" in *Dr. Who* fandom whooshed out of my mind like air from a blown tire.

In the end I stayed at the convention and tried to enjoy it, but I couldn't. I couldn't think, I couldn't eat, and I sat through the performances like a stone. But going home would have been useless. It was the weekend, and there was no way I could begin to make all the arrangements like getting sick leave from my job and getting a hospital date. It was better to try to keep busy.

So I trusted in God to get me through the weekend, and I asked Enniss to pray for me for extra strength of will and courage. "Stay close to me, dear angel," I asked. "Dear God, help me to sense your love and care for me. It's not so much that I feel afraid, but I feel so lonely."

I finally finished dressing for the costume parade and went downstairs, feeling terribly isolated. Even winning a six-foot inflatable *Tyrannosaurus rex* did nothing to improve my spirits. The plastic dinosaur, with its rows of air-filled teeth, only reminded me of the monster growing inside me. In the end I traded it to a twelve-year-old Spock for a video of *Star Trek* bloopers. The thought of taking a monster back up to my room and having it stare at me all night was more than I could take.

After the costume parade was done, I sat down on a sofa in the hotel lobby, unconcerned that many of the more ordinary guests were staring curiously at me in my fuchsia velvet gown with leg-of-mutton sleeves and three-foot gold collar. My future loomed bleakly ahead of me. Surgery. Pain. Months of convalescence. And no assurance the doctors would "get" It. The voices of fear began to whisper again, and this time they had an even nastier message:

*It's all your own fault. If you had lost weight when you were younger, maybe the cancer wouldn't have developed. If you had gone to your doctor more often, it would have been found sooner.* I began to wonder at that moment if God was punishing me for not taking better care of my health. It was scary to think that the loving God I knew and believed in might actually be "up there" waiting to dump on me for past misdeeds. I could feel my faith shivering, and I began to panic inside.

Suddenly, I realized there was a woman sitting next to me. I hadn't noticed her before. She was a tall, middle-aged woman with short, curly, black hair and dark brown eyes and a flawless café-au-lait complexion. She spoke with a kind of Caribbean accent—I never have figured out which.

"Do you want to talk about it?" were the first words out of her mouth. She spoke softly, in a friendly way, with a small smile on her face.

"I, what, uh, huh?" was my less than articulate reply.

"You're in some kind of trouble, dear, aren't you? I always know these things. It's the way I am. I saw you at the costume contest and I knew you needed help. You were as white as a sheet. Why don't we have some tea and you can talk about it?"

She got to her feet and gave me her hand, and I followed her numbly like a pet spaniel. We walked into the restaurant together, she in her neat pantsuit, me looking like a creature from another planet, and sat down at a table in the corner.

"We'll have a pot of mint tea," she said to the waiter. (Mint tea is my favorite hot beverage, but I had no idea how she knew that; I had never seen her before.)

"Now, dear heart, tell me all about your troubles," she said calmly.

And I did just that, crying and hiccupping and spilling my tea. "What am I going to do?" I finished.

The woman looked into my eyes and took my hands in hers. "You're going to trust in God to get you through this, and you're going to keep your eyes and your ears wide open for all the good lessons you're going to learn," she said seriously. "God doesn't just dump serious illness on people. When it happens, it happens for a reason. Look for the lessons. Ask for help and take help wherever you find it. God is going to heal you, although it may not be the kind of healing you had in mind. Don't beat yourself over the head trying to find out why you developed cancer. And don't be afraid."

9

I stared at her in amazement. There was such quiet conviction in her softly accented voice that I shivered.

"You know, I had an experience long ago, when someone told me never to be afraid," I said. "I believe it was my guardian angel."

She nodded sagely in encouragement, as I told her all about seeing my angel when I was a child.

"You mustn't blame yourself for your illness," she told me as she poured more tea in my mug. "And it's important not to let fear take hold of you. Fear delays healing more than almost anything else. Remember the psalm that says, 'The angel of the Lord encamps around those who reverence him and delivers them.'

"I have to go now," she said, getting up. "But I'll be around the con this weekend in case you need someone to talk to." And with a friendly pat on my back, she left.

I sat there nursing my tea, with her encouraging words of hope floating through my consciousness. An old gospel chorus with the psalm verse she had quoted came to mind, and as songs often are, was so powerful that I found myself humming it over and over. Once again the voices of fear were silenced and went away.

I signaled for the hostess and asked for my check. "No charge." She smiled. "The manager says your costume is so unusual that the tea is on the house."

"Well, thanks, but I should at least pay for—that is, I should pay for my friend's tea," I replied. It suddenly occurred to me that I had never even asked her name.

"I didn't notice anyone sitting with you," the hostess said. "But I wasn't especially paying attention. I thought you came in alone. In any case, the tea is compliments of the management."

I was still so sunk in worry and anxiety that her words almost passed unnoticed. I had put away my bartered videotape in my hotel room when it occurred to me:

—The woman had never even told me her name.
—She knew I was in deep distress even before I told her.
—She not only comforted me, she offered me some practical help—a message of God, from God, consistent with the kind of help God gives us.
—She reminded me again not to be afraid.
—Her work done, she left so suddenly that no one in the restaurant even noticed her.

"Enniss, was that you in disguise?" I asked hesitantly, coming out of my gloom into a world with light.

I felt that his answer was no, and yet not totally so. Then I heard him say, in my heart, *Remember, the Healer of God loves you, too.*

I knew that Raphael is the angel whose name means "healer of God," and I remembered a time in 1979 when I had become aware of his angelic presence in my life. "Dear God, did you send me Raphael with your message of healing?" I asked. "Thank you for such a sign of your love and care." And I thanked Raphael, too, although for some reason I have always preferred to call him Asendar.

(I don't think it's especially important *what* we call our angels, rather, that we call our angels *something*. After all, even names like Michael, Gabriel, and Raphael are just human names. Angels have no lungs and larynxes, so their own language must be totally different from any human means of communicating.)

I got out the convention program and began to write down the words my teatime companion had shared with me: *Trust in God. Keep alert for lessons to be learned. Don't blame yourself. Ask for help. Never be afraid.*

The words were healing in themselves. I could feel myself growing stronger than I had been since I had received the news from my mother. I was still concerned about the future, but I had a deeper sense of being cared for and loved, not only by God directly, but also by the angels sent by God to help me.

"Stand beside me, dear Enniss, and help me to trust in God. Help me stay awake and aware, so I won't miss anything I need to learn. And fight for me against the voices of fear. Thank you for your help, dear servant of God." I spoke to my heavenly guardian with great sincerity, and I put myself under the care of the Healer of God.

The weekend was still tough, though through the help of my angels I was less prone to worry. They saw to it that I was scarcely alone for a minute. Whenever an event was over, someone would come up to me, start an interesting conversation, and then go with me to whatever event I was heading for next. Most of the people were strangers to me, and I never saw them again. God's angels simply sent them into my path, and because I was still so numb inside, I went with the flow. On three occasions these strangers all said the same thing that my teatime companion said: Put your trust in God. Don't be afraid. Don't blame yourself. We're here to help. Try to understand what you were meant to learn through all this.

It was really eerie, but I needed all the repetitions. The message of God through Raphael would never have sunk in otherwise. (Much the same thing happened to me in December of 1992 after I lost my previous job and went into shock [See Chapter Four].) To this day I believe that some of the strangers who came up to me during the convention and, as if they had known me for years, just started conversations or took me to lunch, or sat with me at the talks, were angels in disguise. I believe this not only because they all had the same message for me, but because none of the few friends of mine who were attending the con, and who had been in sci-fi fandom far longer than I, knew any of them. I never saw any of them again at any con I subsequently attended. And, although I later saw photos from the convention that surely included virtually every attendee, none of these secret angels appeared in any photo.

By the time the weekend was over, I was learning in a way I had never experienced to put my trust in God's love and care for me. I had always been very independent, but during the convention I realized in a new way not only how interdependent we all are, but also just how good and wonderful a thing it is to need others. I had known it intellectually, of course, but I had never experienced it in my heart. By the end of the con, even the British actors who were the guests knew I was headed for serious surgery, and they all signed a poster for me. Their support was wonderful. I remember singing to myself the old song Barbra Streisand made famous, "People," how people who need other people are the luckiest human beings in the whole world. It was a healing in itself. I believe that was the lesson I was supposed to learn at the con.

It was harder to deal with the fear after I returned

home. My mother was terrified, and I was concerned for her, because she had a bad heart. I had been able to avoid thinking about the practical realities of doctors and tests and procedures at the con, but now they deluged me, making it all too clear just how serious the situation was.

To make matters worse, my medical insurance company informed me they would not pay for my surgery, because of a technicality having to do with my doctor's hospital affiliation. It took three anxiety-ridden days, and the support of my boss at work, before the medical plan agreed to cover my surgery.

In the meanwhile there were tests, all sorts of procedures designed to determine everything from kidney functions to the location of blood vessels in the area of surgery. All of them added to my overall anxiety. And yet whenever the voices of fear would start to speak, somewhere, someone would come up to me and say, "Don't be afraid." Once it was a radiologist; another time it was a nurse named Quiñones, of whom no one had ever heard. I wrote it all down in my journal so I would remember.

Two days before I was to enter the hospital the surgeon prescribed some very potent antibiotics, which made me violently ill. Even some additional medication didn't cure the condition. I became so sick that the surgeon decided he would have to postpone the surgery because I was badly dehydrated. I knew I couldn't stand the wait for another date for surgery. I was becoming too weak to fight against the voices of fear.

"Dear Lord," I prayed, "even if you won't heal my cancer, please at least send your angel Raphael to heal this reaction to the antibiotics so I won't have to wait for surgery anymore. I just can't take it!"

This time God's answer was Yes. No sooner had I finished the prayer than I felt warmth come into me, first through my hands, then into my shoulders and through-out my body. The spasms in my stomach subsided, the violent cramping faded away. I had the kind of inner calmness that I always associated with the presence of my guardian angel. Within an hour I could eat some crackers and take a little tea. By the end of the day my body was back to "normal."

I took this healing as a sign from God that I was moving along the right path; and the next day I found myself in the hospital, where yet another set of anxieties hit me. More tests, unpleasant procedures, dehumaniz-ing, scary. The surgeon reminding me that, although the probability was small, I could die on the operating table. I signed the releases with a shaky hand.

Late on the night before surgery, I could not sleep. I had prayed, had received the sacraments of my church, and had tried with all my heart to entrust myself to God's loving care, but by one in the morning, the only voices I heard were the voices of fear. I won't repeat the terrible things they said. I only know that I was crying into my pillow, shaking with fear, trying not to let the voices inside, where I knew they would take me over and destroy me.

"Can I help?" said a voice next to me.

I felt a warm hand on my shoulder and I turned over to see a nurse sitting by my bed. I hadn't heard him come in, I was so turned inward.

"I'm so scared!" I cried out in a tight little shriek.

"I'm never going to get through this. I'm going to die! The cancer will have spread too far by now! I'm not going . . ."

"Get hold of yourself," the man said quietly. "None of what you say is true. There's a purpose in everything that happens. You just have to get through this and learn from it. Whatever happens, God won't abandon you. Don't give in to the fear."

I looked at him, my mouth agape in amazement. The same messages that I had been receiving all along the way! Was this another angel?

He smiled at me and handed me the box of tissues and a glass of water. "Here, you'll feel better if you blow your nose."

I did so, calming down more and more with every minute that passed. When I had finally gotten back control of myself, I looked over at him and asked, a little sheepishly, "I don't suppose you're really an angel, are you?"

I remember he gave me a strange look. "I suppose I am," he answered. But as my heart started to beat faster, he added, "After all, we nurses are sometimes called 'angels of mercy,' aren't we?" He smiled and reached up to turn out the light over my bed in a very ordinary way. "You'd better try to get some sleep," he said, "or your real angel will be put out."

I realized at that moment just how exhausted I was. I had been trying to stay awake because I was afraid to go to sleep, just as I had tried to keep from sleeping when I was a child, the night my guardian angel came to release me from my fears of death. Now I was no longer afraid. I closed my eyes briefly, just for an instant; when I opened them again, the nurse was gone. But in his place was a luminous glow, an unearthly light not unlike what I saw as a child. I only saw it for a moment; then it faded away.

What had I seen? Was it a compassionate and wise nurse on the night shift—or was it literally an angel? Had I imagined it? Did I fall asleep and dream? Could I have seen angels in my dream? I couldn't separate out what happened.

"Was that you, Enniss, or was it Asendar?" I asked.

*Go to sleep, child. God loves you, and so do we, God's servants. Do not be afraid.*

And in that moment, all anxiety left me totally. I felt as though I were swimming in an ocean of peace, floating on a sea of love. I was filled with such serenity that I knew I had, by God's grace, conquered the voices of fear, that they had no more power to disturb me ever again, that they had been defeated and would not return. Even more, I knew that, just as my spirit had been healed because I had tried to follow God's message to me through the divine messengers, the angels, that my body would also be healed in turn.

I knew my angel would guide the hands of the surgeons, and I slept.

What happened next is something I can't vouch for totally, but deep in my heart of hearts I believe that my angels were involved. The reason I'm not perfectly sure is that the minute I was awakened in the morning, the nurse came with some medication that spaced me out. It was designed to reduce anxiety. I tried to tell the nurse that I was no longer in the slightest bit anxious, but she insisted, so I let her give me the injection. (She told me afterward that I spent the next hour limp as a leaf, my eyes closed, singing folk songs at the top of my lungs!)

Still, by the time the orderlies came to wheel me to

surgery, I was quite aware of my surroundings. I said hello to the two surgeons, my regular ob-gyn doctor and a surgeon who specialized in difficult cancer cases. They had no objections to my offering a prayer and entrusting all of us to the love of God. Afterwards I lay back quietly and asked God for my angels to remain very close to me . . .

. . . and the next thing I remember is beginning to return to consciousness in a dimly lit recovery room. For a moment I felt so light, so free, so full of an energy-charged light that I was amazed. I knew I had just come through major surgery. *You shouldn't feel so good,* I smiled to myself.

And then I realized that I was no longer in my body. In fact I was looking down on my body from a point about three feet away. I saw a very white face with an oxygen mask, the rest of my body covered with white sheets and blankets. The scene was so monochromatic it could have been shot with black-and-white film.

I looked down on myself, astonished, but certainly not afraid. It was as if I could see through the covers, see through my body itself, and see everything that had been done to me. I had the feeling that this was the only way I could experience and understand what had happened.

And as I watched, a being of light, whose colors contrasted vividly with the hospital white all around me, moved toward me from behind the bed. I did not see any particular form, the way I had as a child, but I knew instantly that this was Raphael, the Healer of God. The light being embraced my body with its rays; in fact, it seemed as if my body absorbed the light; and I saw my face relax and the corners of my mouth twitch as though

I were smiling. Then I felt my consciousness being pulled back into my body, and I felt a tremendous heaviness. I had never before felt so clearly how our spirits are tied to our bodies. It seemed as if I were an animated block of cement. I couldn't even open my physical eyes.

Whether I actually opened them at some point, or whether what happened next took place in my heart, I don't know, but I saw the angelic light surrounding me. It seemed to me like brilliant, emerald green light, with edges of yellow and gold, and it felt so reassuring that I wanted to sing. And I did sing, although not as I had when the nurse had given me the tranquilizer! Instead, I seemed to sing along waves that were not sound waves but light waves. I felt as though I were singing colors, rather than notes. Later I realized it had many things in common with something I had experienced years before, which I have described in *Touched by Angels*.

And the most extraordinary thing was that the angelic being I knew to be Raphael was singing with me in songs beyond words, the "tongues of angels" that St. Paul speaks of in 1 Corinthians 13:1. At first I wanted to be silent and listen to the music that was far more elaborate than mine could ever be. But as I hesitated, a bright light, like a glowing purple diamond, filled my sight, and a voice said, *Sing!*; and I sang. It seemed to me that Raphael was healing something within me, and that our prayers (for I felt we were worshiping God) were being poured out like a torrent of musical colors before the Most High.

Then I heard Raphael sing a color I had never heard before, and the angel painted a picture in my mind that sang, *God has healed you* in twenty-part harmony.

19

And with that I went back to sleep, not to wake up for what seemed like hours.

I know that when all of this occurred, I was still under the influence of the anesthetic from surgery. I know that I was receiving intravenous narcotic painkillers, which produce greatly altered mental states. I know that no one can confirm what I experienced. I can't even describe how music can be colored, or how light can emit notes that heal.

But I believe that Raphael's visit was no drug-induced hallucination. I believe that God sent the ancient archangel of healing not only to produce some beneficial effect in my body, but to open my mind and my spirit in some way to enlightenment about the ways in which God works through the angels for our healing.

After I recovered, I spent much time meditating on the experience, and it seemed totally consonant with what I know of how angels work in our lives. I've described the aspects of angelic discernment most fully in *Touched by Angels*, but I will say here that during this encounter, the angel brought love and confidence, clarity and enlightenment, love and a deepening of my faith in God. The experience helped me grow spiritually and made me more thankful to God for all the blessings I had received. All of these fruits are the kinds of things we expect when God sends an angel to us with a message.

When I woke, my surgeon was standing beside the bed. "Your cancer was serious, Miss Freeman," he began. "We had to do a radical hysterectomy. But the cancer did not appear to have spread beyond the wall of the uterus. It certainly appears that we were able to get it all."

"I already know," I murmured sleepily. "But thank you for telling me." I did know; the visit of Raphael confirmed for me that I would be all right. And I went back to sleep.

I spent two weeks in the hospital getting over the surgery. I had been on the operating table for six hours, while the lab biopsied various organs and tissues. For at least a week, I was too sick to do much, and I was receiving pain medication around the clock.

But I was learning lessons, just as the angels God had sent to me reminded me I needed to do. I learned about patience, about compassion, about caring. I was learning about friendship. I was learning just how deep my mother's love for me was. I was learning how healing it can be to depend on the strength of others when one's own isn't enough.

I also believe that my angels provided insights that helped me heal faster than I otherwise would have. Case in point: hospital food.

For the first three days after surgery I was fed intravenously. And then one bright morning, an aide brought in a tray. "You can have clear liquids now," she said cheerfully. She took off the lid and revealed a cup of tea, some chicken broth, some cranberry juice cocktail, and something red that quivered as she poked it.

I looked at the food, hungry, and yet . . . I heard my angel's voice inside that said, *You don't want to eat that. It's not good for you; it won't help you heal.*

"Why not?" I asked, surprised. After all, it was *hospital* food. It was supposed to be good for you. But Enniss didn't respond, a sure sign that God expected me to use my own wits to find the answer.

The aide left the tray and I stared at the red and brown

foods. Then I remembered something I had read while preparing for the surgery, to the effect that sugar and salt are hard for a stomach that has been antibiotic-ed to death to deal with. The chicken broth was mostly salt, and the juice drink and Jell-O were almost all sugar. When there were no friendly bacteria in the stomach and intestines, sugar just decayed and turned into painful gas. I certainly didn't want that pressing against my incision.

So when the aide came back, I told her that I didn't want the tray. She just assumed I wasn't hungry yet, but when I turned down lunch, too, the dietitian came in. I explained my reasoning. "Could you just bring me some real broth, not something made from a cube of salt, and some plain pineapple or papaya juice?" I asked.

It took some doing, but in the end the dietitian agreed to get me some liquids without salt or sugar. And what happened was truly positive: I never experienced any of the intestinal problems all the nurses assured me were the inevitable lot of postsurgical patients like me. Following my angels' advice prevented problems and enabled me to heal faster and more easily.

As I write this chapter, it has been more than seven years since my surgery. But the lessons God sent the angels to teach me about healing have been with me ever since. These principles make up the simple and beautiful premise of this book: that God wants all of us to be whole, and that our angels are always working to make us aware, not only of our need for healing, but of ways in which we can heal our lives:

○ Always trust in God, for the Source of all that exists is intelligent, loving, and caring, and wants us to be whole. God's angels minister to us that loving and caring and healing.

○ Realize that in all things on this planet we are students, and we have a great many lessons to learn, including lessons having to do with healing. Our angels can be powerful teachers, if we have the humility to listen.

○ Never go on blaming yourself for aspects of your life in need of healing. Accept responsibility where it is appropriate and learn to forgive yourself, but don't let any being, human or fallen angel, lay a guilt trip on you. The God of the universe loves you so much that the divine became human in the person of Jesus, and has even given you into the care of the angels. Who could ask for more?

○ Reach out for help in healing, including expert help from health-care professionals and the support of friends and relatives. Lean on God's help, from whatever source, and listen for the help that God's angels bring from their Source.

○ Never, ever, yield to fear. Never! Even more than guilt, it is the thing that can most delay your healing. Many kinds of emotions and thoughts can affect our bodies or spirits, but fear can paralyze not only our bodies, but our minds and souls as well, and can turn us so far inward we cannot reach out for help or learn valuable lessons.

I have tried to follow these simple principles in my life, and I can testify to the fruits I have discovered. These principles, and the attitudes that I have learned to associate with them, have enhanced my ability to understand what my angels communicate to me in the name of God. I have learned more lessons as a result than I can begin to describe. And I firmly believe that the more we can follow these principles that I have learned, the more we can heal our lives, by the grace of God, through the ministry of the angels.

## Chapter Two

# How Angels Help Us Heal Our Lives

*[And Raphael said:] God sent me to heal you. . . .*
*As for me, when I was with you I was not acting*
*on my own will, but by the will of God.*

—Tobit 12:14, 18

 e are all wounded. It's a sad fact, but true. Not a single person on Earth today will leave it without being wounded during their lives. Not a single person on Earth today will leave it without wounding someone else. That's the bad news.

The good news is that we are all meant to be healed and to heal not only ourselves and each other, but our planet. God, the loving Source of all that is, wants us to be healed, to be whole. We were never meant to be crumbs, but a whole loaf.

I believe that healing is a partnership that involves ourselves, the God who caused us to be, other human beings, especially enlightened, skillful, trained health-care professionals—and our angels. None of them can substitute for another, except God. All of them have special gifts. In my experience, most healing involves all of them.

One of my favorite ancient texts on healing is from the book of Sirach, Chapter 38. It reminds us that healing involves work on our part, both external, in seeking professional help, and spiritual, in turning away from the darkness and to the Light:

> *My child, when you are ill, do not delay,*
> *but pray to the Lord to heal you.*
>
> *Give up your faults and direct your hands rightly, and cleanse your heart from all sin.*
>
> *Offer a sweet-smelling sacrifice, and pour oil on your offering.*
>
> *Then give the physicians their place, for the Lord has created them; do not let them leave you, for you need them.*
>
> *There may come a time when recovery lies in the hands of physicians,*
>
> *For they, too, pray to the Lord that they be given success in diagnosis and in healing, for the sake of preserving life.*
>
> *God has given them skill so that the Divine might be glorified in its marvelous works.*

Although angels are not specifically mentioned in this particular passage, they have played an important role in healing—whether the mind, the spirit, the body, or relationships—for as long as the human race has recorded their visitations. By sharing with us God's knowledge and wisdom, they help us come to understand our need for healing better, so we can seek the appropriate help. But what do we mean when we speak of angels?

Some people believe that angels are just thoughts or fantasies, or the spirits of people who have left this world and evolved. I believe—and I feel that both theory and experience bear this out—that angels are another race of sentient, intelligent beings who dwell all around us, but who remain unseen for the most part. I think their invisibility may be due to many things: their own spiritual nature, perhaps, or the limitation of human vision to certain spectra. But it is clear that with an increasing frequency, they are letting themselves be visible to our race.

Angels are far older than we are; in fact, it appears that they were around even before the earth coalesced out of the dust particles that surrounded the sun. They are social creatures with responsibilities and personalities, a sense of purpose and organization. Their society is a peaceful one, unmarred by evil of any kind. They live in love and joy, because their society is centered in the heart of the divine.

Angels serve God, and God is the source of wholeness, integration, preservation, health, and growth for all that exists. For this reason, angels not only seek to live and grow perfectly in their own realm, they earnestly want us to be whole as well. And that is what healing is about—the search for wholeness, not just for our bodies, but for our souls and our minds, our spirits, our relationships, and for the environment around us. Their work with our bodies is most easily apparent, but healing for the mind and spirit, healing for relationships between people and nations, and healing for our environment are just as essential, and just as important to the angels.

Why do angels care about us so much that they take the time and effort to manifest themselves to us? After all, their society is perfect—why should they concern themselves with our problems?

I believe it is because, from the very beginning of our race, angels were appointed as our guardians, to watch over us constantly, from conception until we leave this world and enter the dimension where they live, which is called heaven or paradise or the Kingdom of God. Part of their reason for existence is to help us grow and be healed.

The angels are our companions on the journey—guides, aides, even nurses. I think there's a special connection between nursing and what the angels do; I don't think it's coincidental that nurses are referred to as "angels of mercy." After all, the word *nurse* itself derives from roots that imply far more than care of the sick. The root meaning involves the idea of nourishment, of basic care, of concern for the total well-being of the other, and that's what angels and health-care professionals do.

But angels are working with us for our healing not only because it's in their "blood," so to speak, but because they love us and they know we need help. They want us to be healed, to grow, and to evolve. And from what I've seen, we need all the help we can get. We're in deep trouble overall as a race, and our current level of wisdom is insufficient to meet our need for healing.

As Sirach points out, when we have medical problems, we need to take advantage of all the healing avenues open to us for our bodies, from the divine to the doctor. But just as much as physical healing, we also need healing for our spirits. More people than ever feel spiritually starved. We know that our spiritual well-being affects our bodies and vice versa, so we cannot ignore this essential part of ourselves. Our relationships are in deep trouble, too; more marriages are ending up in divorce than ever. And finally, we are so out of touch with the planet we live on and from which we draw our lives that great parts of it are in jeopardy from our misuse of resources. Our whole planet is crying out for healing.

The angels want to help. Behind the scenes, they ceaselessly carry out their divinely assigned tasks, watching over us and all life on Earth. But they can help most effectively when we are conscious of them and try to work with them.

How do our angels help us to heal? First of all, I don't think they often break through the clouds and wave a celestial wand over us. They're too gentle for that. Their behind-the-scenes inspirations are mostly designed to help us heal ourselves, to encourage us toward avenues of healing. And not only that, it's not really in God's plan for them to interrupt our lives, overwhelm our free will, and impose healing on us. After all, we can and should seek healing through others with the gifts and training to know what ails us.

Angels work at the most basic level, healing the deepest anguish of the human heart: the feeling that we are ultimately alone in the world. We feel isolated and lonely, and it's not necessary. Each of us has a guardian angel who works with us as much as we will allow—and almost certainly other angels as well, who come at different times and in different circumstances as we need their help.

Because of these celestial companions we are never alone, and the more we can realize this, the more we can be healed of the most basic pain there is: the pain that

29

comes when we feel isolated, lonely, and cut off from human society. I know I was a fearful, isolated, agoraphobic child until my angel came and let me know that I am never alone, that angels are reminders of God's love for us.

The minute you speak to your angel for the first time, you will never be alone again, because our angels are always with us. No matter where you are as you read this, you are surrounded by angels. Your room, your office, your garden, are filled with angelic presences.

And once you have the security of knowing you are loved and accompanied by your angel, your relationships with others can grow, and, if they have grown bent, can be straightened out.

When we work with our angels for healing, we must understand that our angels always want us to be healed. There's no question that they see our wholeness as a necessary goal. But that doesn't mean that *our* timetable or agenda is the right one, or that the healing *we* would like is the healing that is best for us at the moment.

Healing is always a matter first of all of learning lessons. I remember one day when I was busy running errands in preparation for a workshop I was giving. The traffic was murder, and it seemed to me as if all the bad and careless drivers with attitude problems had been put right in my path just to annoy me. As I pulled into my driveway, I was still fuming over a guy who had cut me off on the highway. My ego was in serious need of some healing!

As I got out of the car, I felt a strong sensation of pain and tightness in my neck and shoulders. *Oh, great, just what I need*, I said to myself. I reminded my guardian angel, whom I call Enniss, about the workshop, and I asked him if he could somehow heal my neck problem so

I could concentrate better on my preparations. But nothing happened, no sensation of warmth, no easing of the stiffness. I went inside, scarcely able to turn my head.

It was then that Enniss reminded me about how I get impatient so easily on the road, and as I thought about it, I realized that I had created the neck problem myself. I had been too busy, hurrying around, full of tension, to notice. So I took some time to relax my whole self and consciously to give up my resentments at the other drivers, recognizing that my mind needed healing even more than my body. And when I had finished, I realized that my neck was no longer especially stiff and sore. I had thought my need was for physical healing, but Enniss knew better. I was most grateful.

I have worked hard to get to know Enniss, at least a little, for more than forty years. During that time I have benefited from his healing on many occasions, as we all do from our guardian angels, whether we know it or not in this world.

As I said, very often in our quest for healing we must resign our own agenda in favor of God's. I don't believe that God makes us sick in order to teach us "lessons" about life. I certainly don't believe that illnesses come as punishment from some vengeful divine being. A folkie friend of mine wears a T-shirt that has the equivalent of the colloquial phrase "sh-t happens" in a number of world religions. Some are apropos, some are funny, and some make me wince, including the "Catholic" one that reads, IF SH-T HAPPENS TO YOU, YOU DESERVE IT. I'm sure that in any religious system—including my own—there are people who believe that, but I don't.

However, I do believe that when we fall ill physically, or when we lack wholeness in our spirit or a relationship,

31

the healing the angels bring us from God is meant to do more than simply restore us to where we were before we became ill. Healing is meant—like all of God's gifts—to teach us something valuable, whether it is love or wisdom, serenity, patience, acceptance, anger (the sort that helps us fight our way to health), or humility. Healing is meant to move us farther down the path of life. I think that is one reason why God so often mediates healing through the angels: they are messengers who come to us with communications of wisdom that help us grow. They are teachers.

I have always felt that we should not necessarily view physical illness or wounds of spirit as terrible events from which we should flee in horror. I have learned through what I have experienced in my life that even our wounds, our diseases, our conditions are opportunities for grace. While we seek healing, whether through natural or supernatural means, we should keep the eyes of our spirits open for lessons to be learned.

When I was in graduate school I held down six part-time jobs at one point, trying to earn enough money to pay my way. I directed three church choirs, gave private piano lessons, and taught music at a local Catholic grade school, in addition to teaching undergraduates in the theology department at Notre Dame. Of course, I was also working on my graduate degree in theology.

I came down with the flu one day, a miserable flu that left me feeling just dreadful, but I pushed on, trying to ignore it. When the flu was over, I was saddled with such a bad cold I thought my head would explode. The cold medicines made one sleepy, so I ignored them, too. The cold lasted for weeks. And when it was nearly finished, I was so run down that I got some sort of infection. I wound up flat on my back in bed, with a friend from the music department coming in several times a day to make me soup and tend my needs. He was an angel (not literally, of course).

It was only when I was thoroughly sick and had to cancel everything I was doing for a while that I could hear Enniss saying to me, *Too many frying pans, not enough burners.* It was a funny statement, but I could finally see how I had made myself sick by ignoring the lessons of moderation that were all around me. (I've always been a bit compulsive.) So I tried to relax. I asked Enniss to obtain a gift of healing for me, but it was clear at once that the answer was no. *What's wrong with healing in the ordinary way?* Enniss asked.

It took me a full week just to be able to get out of bed. In the end I had to quit most of my jobs, and I had to postpone my candidacy exams, too. But the lessons I learned about personal pride and the vanity associated with self-sufficiency were invaluable.

## Asking for Healing

Of all the things we ask for ourselves from God, healing is probably the most common. But how do we ask when we want help in this way? When we need healing (which is just about always, if we think of healing as wholeness), we can approach it in a number of ways:

○ We can do nothing and hope whatever it is will go away.

○ We can seek help from others with abilities, knowledge, or gifts appropriate to our need—specialists in the health-care professions.
○ We can ask God directly for healing.
○ We can ask our angels to mediate the healing of God to us.

All of these methods, except the first, are useful ways to approach our situation.

Seeking help from others is the way we most often go about trying to heal ourselves. When our problem is physical, we may need to go to the medical doctor trained in Western medicine or seek out someone trained in other healing disciplines. We reach out to the knowledge and wisdom of another human being who understands where we are wounded and how we can heal. Sometimes the healer applies body medicine, sometimes spiritual medicine—I always feel that the best healer is one who can apply both, since every need for healing involves our entire being.

Of course we can also ask God to give us directly either an immediate release from whatever our situation is, or to give us the direct infusion of wisdom and enlightenment we need to heal ourselves. Whenever I recognize a need for healing in my life, whether it is in my body, mind, spirit, or a relationship, I never ask God directly for anything at first except for understanding and wisdom. There are always important lessons to learn, and very often our main need is to grow in wisdom so we can learn them.

But most often, God does not miraculously deal with the illnesses and conditions in our lives. Instead, God points us back into more usual means of healing. That is what happened to me when I learned I had cancer. God said no when I asked for a miracle, and healing came through the hands of a great many skilled and compassionate doctors and nurses and other health-care professionals. But even if God will not be our medical specialist, God will always heal us of the fear and anxiety and worry that so often accompany our needs for healing.

I believe that above all other spiritual help, including that of the angels, we must speak directly to God, because we come from God and we return to God. Sharing in the divine life is the destiny we must all aim toward, just as the angels aim to immerse themselves more deeply in the divine Vision. How can we hope to know our own destiny and understand what motivates the angels in all they do if we do not seek God?

Asking our angels for healing is a bit more complex than asking for healing from either God or our fellow humans. I do not believe that angels act as independent agents in healing us. I have never felt that in any of the many cases when Enniss has responded to my needs for healing that he was responding as a free agent, who decided on his own about healing me. I have always felt, as I do in all things concerning him, that his only concern is that God's will be done on earth, as it is in heaven.

I believe that angels are servants of God, that their whole society is utterly focused on the divine; and that their will is totally absorbed in carrying out the plan of God. Our guardian angels are given incredible insight into that plan insofar as it concerns each of us. I believe that, in a limited way, they may even know some of the future of each of their wards. God shares with each angel all of the wisdom and knowledge necessary to guide us into the paths of wholeness.

When I ask Enniss's help, I ask him to be a partner with me in God's plan for the healing of my life. I tend not to ask him for absolutes, like, "Please zap my relationship with so-and-so, who always looks down her nose at me, so that she suddenly changes her tune." No one learns any lessons that way. Rather, I ask him to be my teacher, and to share with me what insight God has given him for my life.

I believe that, like any faithful servant, my guardian angel has a remarkable latitude in the way he carries out his work in my life. I don't believe that Enniss asks God's permission every other second to love me, to help me, to teach me. He already knows what he should do and how he should do it, because that is his nature. But I do believe that his "heart" is so in tune with God that he could never do anything for me that was not in my best interests. I have faith that the healing help I receive from Enniss is not so much his, but God's help, mediated through my angel.

I want to say that I'm not afraid of the term *mediator*. Many people in the Christian tradition associate the word only with Jesus, who is spoken of in the New Testament as *the* Mediator between God and humanity. But mediator simply means someone in the middle who acts, and in that sense, angels are mediators. In fact, angels are called mediators by the suffering Job, who continued to suffer because he would not learn the lessons he needed to learn. The difference between angel and human mediators is that human mediators arbitrate disputes, problems, quarrels; angelic mediators deal in peace, understanding, kindness—and healing.

# How Do Angels Bring Healing?

Many dynamics are at work when healing through our angels takes place.

## Miracles

We tend to throw the word *miracle* around in a most sloppy fashion these days. Within the Christian tradition, which seems to have coined the word, a miracle is an occurrence that requires the suspension of some natural law. It is much more than something unusual or difficult.

The problem with calling events miracles is that we really don't understand yet just what natural laws are. It may well be that spontaneous cures we have called miracles involve some hidden recuperative power within our bodies and souls that we just have not tapped into yet. Tens of thousands of people have been healed of illnesses and medical conditions at Lourdes, the pilgrimage sanctuary in France where the Virgin Mary appeared to Bernadette Soubirous more than a century ago, yet only a relative few have, after intense scientific scrutiny, been labeled miracles by the Catholic Church. In fact, more than 200 accounts of appearances by the Virgin have been reported in the past century; the Catholic Church has declared only eight of them worthy of credence.

Does this mean that I do not believe in miracles? No—I believe in them absolutely. The God who is behind all the laws of nature is certainly free to suspend those laws. The New Testament is full of miracles performed directly by Jesus, by Jesus' followers in his name, and even by angels. The instantaneous healing of a man born blind, the raising of a man who had been dead and buried for three days, the curing of a man diagnosed with leprosy— what can these be but miracles?

I guess what I'm getting at is this: If our angel were to heal a broken bone in the twinkling of an eye, would it be a miracle? Perhaps it would be from our perspective; after all, it is against what we know of nature for a broken bone to regrow in an instant. But natural law for an angel obviously means something different, as they have a different nature. They appear to be able to manipulate matter as we manipulate the air in our lungs to voice our language. If an angel heals us, no matter how awesome it may seem to us, the angel may just be acting according to its nature.

I have interviewed many people who have been healed by angels, and few of the healings would qualify as miracles, even by human standards. But all of the healings were true wonders, and "wonder" is actually the root meaning of the word *miracle*. The Latin term *mirare* means "to look at with wonder or admiration." What else can we do in the face of healing? When a bitter, hate-filled, terminally ill woman is visited by her angel, and is transformed into a loving, wise, and peace-filled terminally ill woman, what is that but a wonder? When a man about to kill himself in despair over his life sees an angel and is healed so that he devotes the rest of his life to helping others, isn't that a miracle, in its own way?

## Direct Healing

Direct healing differs from healing through miracles only as a matter of degree. I think such healings are mostly matters of our physical bodies or external circumstances. Healings of our mind, spirit, relationships, cannot be done directly because they first require some growth or enlightenment on our part. But angels can, and do, step in to remove physical conditions that hinder us from carrying out our purpose.

Touch, heat, and light are the three vehicles that angels seem to use most often in healing us directly. Many people testify to the healing touch of an angel.

Some years ago, a friend of mine was in dreadful pain from a broken arm that simply would not heal. Her arm had been in a cast for nearly six months, and the pain was so great that her spirits were very low. The doctors were discouraging—they could offer no more help. "Even if it eventually heals, it will always be weak," her orthopedist said.

Now, my friend had been a very active woman. She had a large family of children, and painting had been her hobby and pastime.

One night, after the children were in bed, she sat in the living room with her husband, trying to read, but the throbbing pain reduced her to tears. "Dear Jesus," she prayed, "I just can't take this anymore. Would you please send your angel to heal me? I would be so grateful."

She felt her spirits lift, and calmness and a sense of reassurance filled her so that her depression and fear went away. "I took it as a sign that healing would come," she said. And because her outlook had been healed, she could deal with the pain, as bad as it was, and not let it overwhelm her.

The next evening she was again sitting in the living room, praying quietly, when she felt a sudden surge of heat and warmth in the broken arm. "It was as though someone had touched me with a hot finger, and the touched had welled outward and through my arm," she said. And when the sensation of heat had faded, she realized that she was no longer in pain. She curled her fingers and flexed her wrist, and she felt fine.

A couple of days later, still feeling no pain, she went back to her orthopedist for more X rays. They showed that the bone had knitted completely, and the doctor removed the cast. To this day, my friend believes that her angel healed her broken arm.

I could tell many similar stories, just changing the name to Jack or Teresa or Loreen, and the healing to a migraine, a sprained ankle, or a terrible cold. In most cases people feel a touch, an embrace, a warmth, and they know in their hearts that a healing has been done. The fruits of their confidence are soon made manifest.

Healings with angelic light seem, in my experience, to be more often connected with healings of the mind and spirit than of the body. It's as though the angel realizes that we associate light and enlightenment, and that the sensation of being bathed in light enables us also to accept a greater wisdom and understanding about our situation. When physical healings include the angelic light, there's usually some kind of wisdom being communicated as well, to help put the physical healing in perspective.

## Indirect Healing

In my experience, angels far more often help us to heal ourselves than heal us directly. An angel's task is to be our spiritual guardian, to teach us, to lead us to God, and to share with us the spiritual qualities we need to do that. I once had a bad head cold that went on and on. It made me just want to curl up and play dead. I asked Enniss if he could heal it for me because it was a nuisance. He just laughed gently. I could almost hear him saying, *Stop being lazy, dear heart; get up and call your doctor. Make some chicken soup. Go buy some zinc lozenges.* I remember at first being a bit miffed at such cavalier treatment. It may only have been a cold, but it was a bad cold and I felt rotten. But I realized that the cold wasn't my problem; it was my lethargy, my laziness. The cold had brought it to the surface, and Enniss was right. I didn't need a wave of an angelic magic wand; I needed to do the usual.

So I got up and washed and dressed, and I did feel a bit better. I called my doctor, and made an appointment. I put some chicken in the microwave to defrost and started making soup, and on the way to the doctor's I bought some zinc lozenges. My perspective improved immensely as soon as I stopped feeling so sorry for myself, and the cold was easier to deal with. The doctor's prescription improved the symptoms. The soup eased the congestion, and the zinc lozenges seemed to stop the sore throat that was coming on.

In short, I was able to heal myself, once I had listened to my angel. Direct healing was inappropriate, so Enniss helped in another way.

Angels also help us to heal ourselves by bringing us

knowledge. Knowledge means factual information, and angels often provide just what we need when we need it. One extraordinary example of just that is a story I heard many years ago when I was still in high school:

✳ ✳ ✳

## Angel on the Radio

A FRIEND OF MY FATHER'S once told a story about a time he went to Canada with a friend to photograph wildlife. They were staying in a cabin that belonged to a third party. They had electricity from a generator, but no phone, and they were far away from "civilization." The two men had parked their car as close as they could get, which is to say a good hour's walk away, and had hiked in.

My father's friend Jim went out to the tall woodpile to get some logs soon after they arrived and accidentally pulled the badly balanced stack of wood over on him. His companion, Walter, hearing the noise, came out and managed to get Jim out from under the heavy logs and inside the cabin. He had no broken bones that were obvious, but his abdomen grew painful and was tender to the touch. They were afraid he might have internal injuries. Jim tried to walk, but he was unable to. Walter got him a blanket and then headed out at a run to bring help. The last thing he did was to turn on the radio to a music station.

"I sat on the bed, hurting real bad," said Jim. "I hadn't the slightest idea what to do to help myself, although I figured that staying real quiet would be a good idea. Walter had left a bottle of bourbon on the table, and some tea from breakfast. I just sat there for a while, listening to the music from the radio across the room and being a bit irritated. The music was full of static because the radio station was badly tuned."

After a bit, Jim reached for the bottle of bourbon, hoping to ease his pain. He was starting to feel shaky. Just as he put the bottle to his lips, another radio station overlapped the music station and he heard a talk-radio program instead. It appeared to be a news or informative show of some kind:

". . . alcohol the worst thing for the ruptured spleen," a voice was saying. "It only dilates blood vessels more." Then the voice faded and the scratchy music filtered back in.

Jim put down the bottle in amazement. How had such information come just at the time he would have needed it? He sat back, feeling cold and increasingly shaky, and drank some hot tea from the Thermos instead.

Just then the music faded out again, and the overlapping station came in, this time as clear as a bell. "We knew she had a ruptured spleen, so we got her to lie down and covered her well to keep the danger of shock down to a minimum. While we waited for the rescue team to bring the antishock trousers, we raised her legs high to force blood back into the vital organs, and—" The music returned.

Quickly, as if the voice had been speaking just to him, Jim reached out to grasp his woolen hat and down vest. Then he stood up with difficulty, pulled aside the bed covers, and lay down, wrapping himself in the blankets, with his head at the foot of the bed and his legs resting high on the pillows. He drank some more hot tea and prayed for help, the pain becoming almost more than he could bear.

Once again, the music was replaced by the other program. ". . . but she was all right in the end. This is [unintelligible] radio, from Boise."

The next thing Jim remembered was the sound of voices from the paramedics around him in the cabin. "I'm glad he's still with us," said one. "Right, let's put the antishock trousers on him and get him into the gurney," another voice said.

Jim finally woke up for good in the surgical recovery ward. As it turned out, he had not only ruptured his spleen, but had somehow caused a blood vessel connected with his liver to tear, and he had, in fact, broken one of his ribs. But everything had been repaired, and he would be fine.

"It was a close shave," said Walter. "The EMT said that if you had drunk the booze and stayed sitting up, you would probably have passed out and died of shock or internal bleeding. What made you do all the right things?"

Jim explained.

"From Boise?" said Walter. "That's at least a thousand miles away! How could a radio signal travel that far?"

For Jim and Walter, it was just an unexplained but fortuitous event. They never were able to find out what radio station in Boise might have had on a story about a rescue. But I've always known it was Jim's angel, giving him the knowledge he needed to keep his body whole enough to survive until help arrived.

## Healing through Others

Although angels heal us directly, or by teaching us the lessons we need to heal ourselves, they also work through other people. I don't believe that angels can manipulate people or make them do anything they want them to. Our free will as human beings is one of our greatest blessings. But I do believe that angels can and do whisper knowledge and help in the ears of others so that our fellow human beings can help us heal. I think that's why in so many cases we call others "angels." It's not literally true, of course, but I think we often receive the help of people acting under angelic inspiration. If you look at your own life, I'm sure you will find instances where someone came to you, a friend or relative, or maybe even a stranger, and you knew by some means other than our usual ones just how this person needed help in order to heal. I believe that these unusual occurrences are gifts of the Holy Spirit, ministered to us by angels so we can help each other heal.

This is a two-way street, of course. We can receive the benefit of the angelic whisper in a friend's ear, or we can be the healing voice to another through the inspiration of our own angels. We must become more and more open to the voice of the angel, whether ours or another person's, that speaks to us to inspire us in ways that help the other person heal. If we want to live lives worthy of the daughters and sons of God, we can never close off our hearts in fear or selfishness to the message that enlightens us to bring healing to others. All of us can be and probably already are instruments of God's healing through the angels, and that is the way it should be.

I don't offer any kind of angelic counseling ministry because I am not trained in the helping professions, but nonetheless in informal situations I am often face-to-face with people in search of healing. I never talk to them without first asking Raphael and the angels of healing, including our guardian angels, to speak to both of us and let needs for healing be honestly expressed. I ask my angel and the other person's angel for the insight and wisdom from God that I may need in order to help the other person, and I try to be very aware of and very sensitive to the grace of God that comes to me through my angels.

Healing is not a case of being passive and letting something be done to us by or through the angels. Rather, it involves a tremendous amount of activity on our part, of receiving and giving of energies, of releasing egotism and accepting humility. And we should ask for our angels to intervene for our healing and that of others and of the world. We need to build relationships not only with our own angels, but with the angels of healing, for beyond our own guardians are special angels, not to mention mighty archangels, who have been given particular responsibilities in the area of healing.

## Chapter Three
# The Angels of Healing

*From time to time an angel would trouble the water, and the first person who entered the pool would be healed.*

—John 5:5

ngels have been associated with healing since antiquity. It's not a new role for them, although some people are just discovering how much they want to work with us so we can heal our lives. I believe that whenever healing takes place in the human heart or body, an angel is present, doing the healing work that God requires.

All of our angels are healers in their own way. Our special guardians know everything there is to know about us, both physically and spiritually. They know our need for healing better than we do, and they are delighted to be asked to help.

In general, I believe that angels do not often heal us directly and instantaneously. They prefer to enlighten us with the grace of God to understand our need for healing.

And once we are aware of our need, they share with us the wisdom and insight we need to take steps to heal our lives, guiding us by God's light. But as we know, angels can step in, when it is part of the divine plan, and perform miracles in our lives.

Working with us to help us heal our lives is something angels do easily and willingly. Angels are not perfect— no creature is—but there is no darkness in their lives that needs healing, no evil that must be turned from in order to live in the Light. Their bodies are not subject to sickness and injury, as ours are. Their intellect is far superior to ours, and it is not complicated and darkened by ego and selfishness, so their knowledge is pure. They all understand the purpose of their existence, which is to reflect back to God as purely as possible the glory God has placed in them. They see God "face-to-face," so to speak, and they want us to know that ineffable joy no less than they, so their dedication to helping us heal our lives is untiring. They want us to have the highest wisdom possible, for wisdom enlightens the intellect, and an enlightened mind knows when healing is necessary and how to seek it, no matter whether the need is for physical healing, emotional healing, healing of relationships, or any other kind of healing.

When our angels work with us for healing, we can know the effects of their help, especially if we are in the process of building angelic friendships with them. We see the progress we are making in any given area, and we know that the wisdom or insight is something we have received from outside ourselves. And the more we work with our angels for healing, the more we will realize that healing comes to us not so much *from* the angels, but from God *through* the angels. As we see ourselves being healed, we will certainly give our angels our deepest thanks, but the glory and praise should be directed to God.


# Our Guardian Healers

Our closest angelic allies in our healing process are our own guardian angels. These ancient beings of light are assigned to watch over us from the moment our life in this world begins. There was a time when I used to believe that this bonding took place when we were born, but now I understand that it begins earlier, when each of us is first conceived. Our angels believe in starting as early as possible!

It is also quite possible that our angels receive some information about us even before our soul and body are brought together. God says to the prophet Jeremiah in the Old Testament, "Before I formed you in the womb, I knew you." Perhaps God shares some kinds of knowledge about us with our guardian angels so that they know all about us long before we leave our mother's womb.

Our own guardian angels are our first and best partners in healing. Not only do they help us on an ongoing basis, but they work with the guardian angels of any human healers we may need to consult. As heavenly physicians, they combine the best of both worlds: general practitioners, in that they know us from top to toe; and specialists, because each one specializes in the care and healing of one particular human being.

In fact, whenever I need to see my doctor or chiropractor, my spiritual director, or anyone whose ministry is healing, I always speak to their guardian angels in advance, asking them to work with the person toward an astute diagnosis and a way of healing that's correct.

I remember one instance of this that happened some years back. I had gone to my chiropractor for an adjustment, and had asked his angel for help. When Paul began the adjustment, he seemed to hesitate, and I asked him why. He explained that, even though there was no logical reason why he should work on a particular area, he just felt strongly that it would help if he did. I told him to go ahead and follow his instincts, and when he was finished, I felt much greater relief than ever before. Afterwards he said it was as if two hands had physically moved his own to a part of my spine he had not thought was involved.

There's no magic involved in asking our angels for healing help, but it is important that we first establish a relationship with them. No doctor will listen seriously to a brand-new patient who walks in off the street and asks for a prescription for a powerful drug. The doctor will insist on establishing a relationship, taking a history, doing necessary tests first.


# A Visualization for Healing


If you have never tried to work with your own guardian angel and the other angels who assist, here is an exercise I heartily recommend. It involves the imagination and our inward, heart-to-heart vision, because there is obviously nothing we can do to compel an angel to appear to us face-to-face. It's a way of speaking creatively with our angels and of inviting them into our lives to heal us.

Sit quietly in a comfortable chair, with your feet flat on the floor, your hands unfolded, and relax your body as much as you can. Close your eyes and breathe steadily and peacefully. You can play some soft instrumental music to cover up background noises like steam pipes and traffic outside. In whatever way you wish, ask God for help in knowing your guardian angel more intimately. Then begin to imagine that your angel is standing in front of you. Your angel is always before you, so all you are doing is trying to visualize what your angel might look like. I don't think there's any way to get a wrong picture; if it helps us communicate with our angel, it's the right picture. In any case, even people who see angels with their physical eyes only see an approximation.

Try to be as detailed as you can about this visualization. See the light that surrounds your angel, that surrounds you, too, as you become aware of her. Look at his face. Do you see the utter peace, the joy, the serenity and wholeness about this being? Reach out your hands and take your angel's hands in yours. Feel the contact being made.

Thank your angel for being there all your life, to lead and guide and inspire you to be the most wonderful person you can be. Then unclasp your angel's hands and relax your own, as your angel puts her hands on your shoulders. Thank him for the strength and healing he shares with you every day, and think about what in your *own* life needs healing. Is it a temporary headache, or perhaps some heartache that won't go away? Decide what you want to lift up for healing.

Then, as your angel lays her hands on your head, say, "I want to be whole in every way. It is in God's plan that all of us should seek healing and wellness. And therefore

Eileen Elias Freeman

I give up this thing that is preventing me from being whole." You should give it a name, like "this headache," or "this fear of falling," or "this constant impatience with others." And then ask your angels for help in healing.

You may ask for instantaneous healing, if you want, but in my experience, angels are more inclined to work toward our enlightenment, so we can understand the causes in our life of whatever needs healing and heal it ourselves. It's rare that they intervene point-blank, but if it's in the great plan for your life, it can and does happen. The fact is that illness, pain, and the like are not random occurrences. They come into our lives to teach us something, and we need to understand what that is before we can work through them and be healed or know how to heal ourselves.

After you ask for help, it's always essential to give thanks. We would be terribly ungrateful to God if we didn't thank our angels for their help in healing. Naturally all things, including healing, ultimately come from God, but if we thank the messenger who comes with flowers for our birthday, even though the flowers come from a friend, not the messenger, how much more should we thank God's heavenly messengers for their help?

I believe we should make this kind of healing visualization a regular practice in our own lives, but just as importantly, we should be calling on our angels for healing of others as well.

I remember one day when I was in Manhattan on my way to see my editor. A man boarded the bus, and it was clear that he was angry and hurt about something in his life. He was bumping into people hard and saying very nasty things. At first I thought to pray that he would just leave or to ask for protection for myself. I realized, of course, how selfish that was, so instead I visualized his angel putting his arms around him and healing him with peace. I asked my own guardian angel to go over and add his healing energies. And I thanked God for wanting his healing. And within just a minute or two, the man sat down quietly, stopped his obscene and hurtful remarks, and opened his newspaper. I could see a change on his face. I knew there was some healing taking place, because, as he rose to leave, he bumped into a man who was standing, and said, "Excuse me."

In addition to our own guardian angels, who are ceaselessly working for our healing, many other angels are known as healers who work in human lives. We should certainly turn to them and ask their help when we seek healing. Most of these angels are known not by name so much as by what they do. I like to think of them not as guardian angels per se, but as specialists who come into our lives when our guardian angels ask for particular expertise. I know that many people call upon these angels directly, but I prefer to ask my own guardian angel to seek out the "specialist" he feels is most suitable for whatever my need for healing is.

# Raphael the Archangel— The Healer of God

Raphael is the ultimate specialist. His name stands out like a brightly shining light in human history, going back to the ancient Near East. The great archangel, one of the Seven who stand before God, according to tradition, has a very special healing relationship with the human race, in comparison with many other angels, who come briefly as messengers or not at all.

Raphael is a mild and compassionate angel who understands human ways well. He is, as his Hebrew name (רפאל) denotes, the healer par excellence: *rapha'* (heals) + *'el* (God). The basic root means more than just physical healing. It includes every kind of mending or fixing or repair, from the darning of socks to the purification of water to fixing defects in products. Other translations from cognate languages include: stitch together, repair, pacify, strengthen, etc. One can see that the essence of the name Raphael involves a "change for the better," whether in regard to one's physical being or spiritual essence, a restoration of something to its original, intended state.

## Raphael in the Ancient Near East

When trying to understand someone's character, whether human or angelic, it is always best to begin with the most ancient written sources for that person. In the case of Raphael, we must go back even before the ancient texts of Judaism, to the city-state called Ugarit (pronounced: oo-gah-reet).

Ancient Ugarit was a powerful political and cultural force in the Near East about 2,300 years before our present era, more than 1,000 years before the wandering Jews found their way into the Promised Land. Located on the

Mediterranean seacoast of northern Syria, Ugarit traded with the world. The people of Ugarit spoke a language closely akin to Hebrew, although they wrote in an alphabetic cuneiform. Their pantheon included the high god El and his consort Atirat, the storm god Baal and his sister Anat, and a number of other divinities.

It also included angels.

The Ugaritic texts that were unearthed at Ras Shamra in 1928 include long and discursive texts on the doings of the heavenly beings. Among these texts are a number that mention the messengers of the gods, who were part of the "divine council" or *puhru ilani*, as it was sometimes called, that advised the reigning divinity, El. These messengers are called by the identical term often used in the Hebrew scriptures for angels: מלאכים, *mal'akim*.

Who were these messengers of ancient Ugarit? What did they do? And why can we call them "angels"?

In virtually every respect, the angels of Ugarit correspond to what the beings we call angels do. First of all, these *mal'akim* were subordinate to the high gods of Ugarit. They did what the high gods told them to do and refrained from acting when told not to intervene. Second, they served as messengers for the gods, not only between one god and another, but also as messengers to the people of earth from the gods. Third, they are described as immortal beings of spirit, not flesh and blood, yet they were also created beings. In fact, one long story, generally titled, "The Birth of the Gracious Gods," describes how two of their number, Shalim and Shahar, were created by the high god El. Fourth, one of their duties was to sing the praises of El and the other ruling deities.

And perhaps most important for our understanding of angels as healers, the angels of Ugarit often came to Earth as the patrons or guardian spirits of individual human beings, and that is how we first meet Raphael.

A number of texts from Ugarit deal with a slightly obscure group of beings called the Rephaim, whose name also derives from the same root as Raphael. Because the Ugaritic texts are broken in several key areas, it is hard to know exactly who they are. It may be a term used of the spirits of those who have died, or of a certain group of such spirits. It may also refer to people on earth whose heavenly protector was the being we call Raphael. In the Hebrew scriptures the term was used of the spirits of the dead in Sheol, the Underworld.

At the head of the Ugaritic Rephaim is a spirit named Raph'a or Rapi'u. His name corresponds precisely with that of Raphael, allowing for differences in languages, just as François and Francisco both mean Francis in French and Spanish. He appears to have some responsibilities in their regard, and they regard him as their patron or special guardian.

The best-known of the Ugaritic Rephaim is Daniel or Dan'el, who was a hero of legendary fame in Ugarit (and whose name and deeds probably come down to us filtered through the Hebrew/Aramaic book of Daniel in the Old Testament). Daniel is called the "Raph'a-man," i.e., the devotee or adherent of Raph'a.

Daniel, according to the story, had no sons, and so he prayed to his guardian spirit to heal his sterility, so that his wife would be blessed with a son to carry on the family. Raph'a apparently took the request to El, the father of gods and humans, who granted the request.

Daniel was instructed, presumably by Raph'a, to perform certain rituals and make certain sacrifices, all of which were common religious practices at that time, and in due course his wife conceived and bore a son.

This is an extraordinary story, for it tells that long before the Jews, the Greeks, or the Persians, an ancient Near Eastern tradition of guardian beings existed, protective, intelligent spirits who watched over individuals and who brought their requests and needs before the high god, who alone had the power to grant them. And the first one we meet by name is Raphael—and he is already associated with healing. Two thousand years later, this same angel of healing would surface in Jewish writings.

## Raphael in Judaism

Most of what we know of Raphael's healing work on Earth comes from two main sources: the biblical (or deuterocanonical) book of Tobit, and 1st Enoch, parts of which are even older than some biblical books (like Daniel, for instance).

### RAPHAEL IN I ENOCH

An ancient Near Eastern collection of documents, attributed to the Jewish sage Enoch, has re-emerged today because of the vast amount of text devoted to the angels this collection contains. It is one of our most ancient sources of information on Raphael.

The Book of Enoch is actually five documents in one, with five different authors, the earliest written about 300 B.C.E., the latest, about 150 B.C.E. It was preserved largely in Ethiopic, and translations into European languages were not made until a mere 150 years ago.

Enoch sprang from a period when religious speculation was at the height of its flowering. The material prosperity of the Jewish community had been destroyed by invaders, and the people took refuge in their faith. And out of that faith, interest in angels mushroomed.

The first section of Enoch, called the "Book of the Watchers," describes extraordinary heavenly journeys taken by Enoch (a pseudonym, of course), during the course of which he was given many revelations about the nature, names, numbers, and responsibilities of the angels. It is Enoch that first names the Four (or the Seven) archangels. Enoch also speculated on what kinds of contact the angels had with humans.

Recently, some modern editions of the texts have been published that suggest that Enoch is a mysterious book full of hidden, forbidden knowledge that only the chosen few can learn. Nothing could be further from the truth. In its day, the Enochian corpus was a best-seller, and it was discussed from Alexandria in Egypt to the Balkans by Christians and Jews alike—and even by Greek philosophers. It's quoted in the Bible in Jude 1:14. It spawned dozens of imitations. Anyone who could read or who frequented places where books were discussed knew about Enoch.

1 Enoch is one of those works that were so influential in their day that they almost made it into the canon of the Jewish scriptures.

1 Enoch is a veritable tour de force of angels. More of them are mentioned by name than in almost any other ancient work. And among them one of the most important ones is Raphael.

Most often in 1 Enoch, Raphael is paired with Michael, Gabriel, and Uriel, to form a group of four angels who were particularly revered in antiquity. Sometimes to the Four are added Phanuel, Saraqael, and Raguel.

We first meet with Raphael in 9:1, where he and the other Three have observed great evil and corruption on earth, on account of the deeds of the fallen angels Azazel and Semhazeh, who have led other angels to seduce humanity with evil. This vision takes place before the great Flood. But those who remained righteous call out to them for help, saying, "Bring our cause before the Most High."

The angels immediately intercede with God for special help for the faithful, and God answers their prayers, giving each angel a different mission. In 10:4ff., God orders Raphael to "bind Azazel hand and foot and cast him into the darkness." He goes on to describe how he is to do this and to detail the punishment for this evil spirit. (This motif of the binding of Azazel recurs in Tobit.) It was widely believed in antiquity that evil spirits caused illnesses, so the connection of the healing angel with the casting out of evil spirits is a logical one. Perhaps we can even make the connection tighter by remembering that one of the root meanings of *raph'* has to do with stitching or binding fabric together with thread. Surely this is related to the concept of binding an evil spirit. Raphael's functions in 1 Enoch are multiple, but all derive ultimately from the meaning of his name.

The Most High then tells Raphael that, once he has bound the demon, he is to "heal the earth which the evil angels have corrupted and proclaim the healing of the earth, that they may heal the plague and that all human beings may not perish." Clearly by this text, Raphael's direct connection with healing is made unmistakable in Enoch. By contrast, both Michael and Gabriel are given some rather stern "search-and-destroy" missions, while Uriel's task is to instruct Noah so he may escape the Flood.

Further on in 40:9, Enoch has a vision of four great archangels, the second of whom is Raphael. His guide tells him that Raphael is "set over all the diseases and all the wounds of humankind." It is here that Raphael's mission as a healer is most clearly set out.

Raphael is specifically called "one of the holy angels, who is over the spirits of men," in 20:3. He is also called a Watcher, a term for angels, either heavenly or fallen, that 1 Enoch is partial to. It may have something to do with an angel's perspective, that is, being a constant observer of the deeds of the human race. The term, however, may also derive from an Aramaic term whose meaning is more appropriately translated as "guardian."

Raphael is appointed as guardian over the spirits of human beings, not specifically their bodies. And this is appropriate for the Healer of God, because all healing begins with the spirit, even healing for our physical ills. Most of the healing we need in our lives is healing of the spirit and of things that touch our spirit, our thoughts, emotions, and relationships.

Chapter 22 contains the account of a journey that Enoch takes with Raphael to view Sheol, which in Jewish thought was simply a sort of neutral waiting place for the spirits of those who have died. After Raphael shows him how the spirits are set apart for judgment or blessedness, Enoch praises God for the revelation. Raphael also shows Enoch the Garden of Eden and points out the tree of wisdom therein (32:6).

This out-of-body experience strikes me as totally in keeping with what we know of Raphael's deeds and duties. After all, the human spirit is an immortal spirit, so it is logical that Raphael should also show Enoch the state of those spirits who have left their bodies. For this reason, Raphael is also associated, within the Roman Catholic tradition, with the spirits in Purgatory, that is, those individuals who, although they lived loving and just lives on Earth, still need further enlightenment and growth and healing before their spiritual "eyes" can open to the glories of heaven. My own guardian angel Enniss calls this place or state the "house of healing" where the wounds of our spirits are mended and spiritual health restored. This house of healing is in the charge of Raphael; I believe that once our own guardian angel escorts us from this world into the next, Raphael will be waiting to help us continue our healing process.

Enoch's great vision of the innumerable multitude of angels who surround the throne of the Lord of Spirits is especially revealing. In 40:9 Enoch hears four of the angels, one praising, one blessing God, one praying and interceding and supplicating on behalf of the human race, and another fending off the evil spirits. It is Raphael who is seen as "blessing the Elect One and the chosen ones who depend on the Lord of Spirits."

Further on in Enoch, both the four angels of the inner circle and the Seven are actively involved in carrying out God's judgments on the earth and on the unrepentant.

So we see that by 300 B.C.E. Raphael was already firmly entrenched in Jewish mystical and apocalyptic literature as the angel of healing par excellence. He was set, not just over diseases and wounds (i.e., natural ills and hurts through violence), but also over healing of the human spirit—whether in this world or the next—and deliverance from evil spirits.

## RAPHAEL IN TOBIT

Tobit is a religious fable that teaches moral and theological lessons. Its anonymous author, most probably an Egyptian Jew, wrote it about 180 B.C.E. Written in Greek, the short work was part of the Bible of the Greek-speaking Jews of the Diaspora. It forms part of the canon of the Old Testament for Catholics and Orthodox Christians, and is considered secondarily canonical for many Protestant Christians. It also contains a wealth of information about how ancient Judaism viewed angels.

The story, which is well written and contains all the elements that make a novel successful, even today, tells how Tobit, a pious but poor and blind Jew, sends his son Tobias to another country to redeem some money he had placed long before with a kinsman. Because Tobias does not know the way, he hires a guide, who turns out to be the angel Raphael in disguise. Raphael, acting in all ways as the Raphael of Enoch would be expected to act, heals Tobit of blindness and drives away the demon Azazel, who was tormenting Tobias's intended wife.

The story, although quaint and full of magical elements, is as modern as anything written today in the way angels are portrayed. The author cleverly writes on two levels: what Tobias perceives, and what Raphael is really causing to happen. For example, at the beginning, when Tobit goes blind, he prays for death; in a far country, Sarah, Tobias's cousin and destined wife, is also praying for death, because an evil demon has slain her bridegroom on their wedding night and everyone is mocking her. At that moment, the story says, "Raphael was sent to bring remedy to them both." So whenever Tobias addresses the angel, he calls him by the name Brother Azariah (his pseudonym); but when Raphael speaks, the text always calls him "the angel."

So when Tobias goes out "looking for a guide," he finds "Raphael the angel standing facing him, although he did not guess he was an angel of God." Obviously Raphael wasn't going to let Tobias get past him!

Tobias asks him who he is, and Raphael says that he is a kinsman who has "come into these parts to look for work." In the course of their conversation, Tobias finds that Raphael (not surprisingly) knows the way to Media. "I have been there many times," Raphael says—perhaps a tongue-in-cheek comment from an angel who can be anywhere he wants at any time!

Since Raphael is in disguise, he does not frighten Tobias or his parents. He wishes the father happiness and tells him: "Take comfort; before long God will heal you." So even at this early point the angel has a message from God—and like most angelic messages, it is one of comfort and joy.

I have always thought that the irony of Tobit asking Raphael if he will be Tobias's guide is especially neat. Here is the consummate guardian angel, already on a divine mission, being politely asked to do just that—and offered "a drachma a day, plus expenses, first class."

And, even more humorous, Tobit's farewell to his son ends, "May God's angel go with you and protect you!" And to his wife, who is sure she will never see her son again, he adds, "A good angel will go with him; he will have a good journey and come back to us well and happy."

Little did he know!

So under the name of "Azariah," Raphael, Tobias, and his dog set out for Media.

I think it is in this early part of the story that we can see just how ancient the idea of personal guardian angels is in Judaism. For the story to have become so immensely popular, the notion must have been universally accepted long before 180 B.C.E., or its readers would have found the concept an odd one. Even more, it appears that Raphael is not just the guardian angel of a single individual; rather he watches over all of Tobit's family and works to heal them all and bring them what, in God's plan, is best for them.

But Raphael is more than a guardian angel; in Tobit, he shows he is also the angel of healing, as his name implies.

The first night out, Tobias goes fishing for his supper and lands a fish that nearly pulls him in. Raphael tells him not to lose it, because it has medicinal values. So, after catching it and frying it for supper, he saves the heart, liver, and gall as the angel tells him to.

Throughout the journey, Raphael is full of good and wise advice. He also acts as matchmaker, telling Tobias to marry the daughter of the man he is going to visit. She has been plagued by a demon, who has killed her seven previous bridegrooms, but Raphael tells Tobias that the fish liver and heart will cause a smoke that will make the demon flee forever.

I think that one of the reasons everything in the story turns out so well is that Tobias always listens to what Raphael has to say. He follows his counsel, and it always stands him in good stead. In the end, it leads to healing, on various levels, for all.

Still, it is clear that Raphael, although a master, sees himself as Tobias's servant. Whenever Tobias tells him to guide them here or bring them there, he does it at once. It is a perfect partnership—the angelic servant guardian and the obedient ward.

Raphael prospers Tobias's journey. The young man, because of the power of Raphael's description, falls so deeply in love with Sarah (whom he has not yet even met) "that he could no longer call his heart his own." He follows Raphael's advice, and as the demon flees from Sarah, Raphael—obviously a being of immense powers—"pursued the demon to Egypt and bound and shackled him at once."

Even beyond the magical qualities of this part, it tells us that the Jews of the period believed that the angels of God had power over evil angels, and that appeals to them for help could be made. We might do well to remember that today. Like Raphael, our guardian angels want what is good for us, what is part of the divine plan, and can go to great lengths to help us in achieving it.

When the happy company arrives back home, Tobias takes the fish gall, as Raphael instructed him, and with it cures his father's blindness. Shortly thereafter, their spiritual "blindness," that is to say, their inability to recognize Raphael as an angel, is also taken away. We should note that Raphael is not the one who actually heals Tobit; it is Tobias who applies the fish ointment to his father's eyes. This is so typical of the way angels work in our lives for healing; so often they stay quite behind the scenes, yet they are the moving force nonetheless. After all, it was Raphael who explained the healing properties of fish gall to the young man Tobias.

I also find it useful to note that throughout the story, as blessing after blessing redounds to Tobias, his thanks go equally to God. It is only at the safe end of the journey that he and his family think to tender their most fervent thanks to Raphael, who has been the prime mover in all the good that has happened to their family.

But Raphael declines any thanks or reward. He says, "Bless God, utter his praise before all the living for all the favors he has given you."

And he reveals more: "When you, Tobit, and Sarah were at prayer, it was I who offered your supplications before the glory of the Lord . . . I was sent to test your faith, and at the same time God sent me to heal you and your daughter-in-law Sarah.

"I am Raphael, one of the seven angels who stand ever ready to enter the presence of the glory of the Lord."

When Raphael reveals his true identity so nakedly, it is then that the humans become afraid, as so often happens. Surely Raphael's appearance must have changed, for all fall on their faces in awe. Raphael then intones the usual angelic greeting: "Fear not!

"Peace be upon you," he continues. "Bless God forever. As far as I was concerned, when I was with you, my presence was not by any decision of mine, but by the will of God; it is he whom you must bless throughout your days, he that you must praise. You thought you saw me eating, but that was merely an appearance and no more. Now bless the Lord on earth and give thanks to God. I am about to return to him above who sent me. Write down all that has happened."

And with that Raphael "rose in the air," and when Tobias rose up, too, Raphael was gone, and they praised the Lord, for "had not an angel of God appeared to them?"

This is clearly the most central thing we learn about Raphael, and, by analogy, about all the servants of God—that they come to us by the will of God and not by their own decision. They expect the respect that such a messenger deserves, but they will take no special thanks or glory for themselves; they refer it all back to God, who sent them. It is something to remember when we try to make the healing partnership we have with our guardian angel a two-way street. It is not. Without God to give depth and breadth to the relationship, it is flat and lifeless.

## RAPHAEL TODAY
Later Jewish mystical literature also placed Raphael as the chief of all healers. In the Zohar, Rabbi Abba said that "Raphael is charged to heal the earth and through him, the earth furnishes a home for human beings, whom he also heals of their maladies." According to the legends and stories of the Jews, Raphael is the angel sent by God to cure Jacob, who injured his hip wrestling with another angel. Raphael is also said to have entrusted a medical book to Noah after the Flood. All these indicate that in antiquity, Raphael was clearly regarded as a healer.

In today's world, Raphael is the angel we turn to for healing on a global scale, as well as for help in dealing with issues of pollution control and recycling, which are ways in which we help heal the Earth. Raphael is also the heavenly protector of pharmacists and those who create medicines and remedies for diseases. There's a verse in the deuterocanonical book of the Bible called Sirach that I think must be especially loved by Raphael.

It says, "God has brought forth medicines from the earth, and the sensible person will not scorn them."

Raphael is considered by many to be the archangel who is over all other guardian angels, who, by the grace of God, assigns their duties and teaches them what guardian angels do. In art, Raphael's symbols are loaves and fishes or an ointment jar; and he is often shown wearing sandals and carrying a staff. Raphael is the patron of pharmacists and herbalists, and was considered the guardian of travelers long before St. Christopher. His traditional feast day is October 24.

For myself, I would also place Raphael among the heavenly guardians or patrons of environmentalists and recycling ventures. As a healer, to whom the command "Heal the earth!" was given in literature written nearly 2,200 years ago, surely he is deeply committed to preserving our planet.

# Michael—Angelic Healer by Water

A second angel associated with healing is Michael, whose Hebrew name (מיכאל) means "Who is like God?" Unlike Raphael, Michael is not in general a healer. His protective duties are far more prominent throughout human history. In antiquity, however, Michael was associated with healing, particularly physical healings, and most particularly with healing through water.

Water is inherently holy to us, because water is essential to life. We can live for months without food, but we die within days for want of water. Rivers and streams were sources of spiritual strength, as well as the means of transportation and a source of food. Flowing waters were seen as emanations of God, bringing life to all, or as the birth waters of the great Mother. In the most ancient times, a god of all the waters—Yamm, Poseidon, Neptune, etc.—was a powerful deity.

From ancient times water has played a most important role in curing diseases and conditions. Hot springs in particular were seen as a special gift from God, and protective spirits or even deities were associated with them. People came from long distances to soak in the hot waters and to pray for healing. Various types of therapies began to be practiced, particularly in ancient Europe. By the time of the ancient Greeks, hospitals and clinics were open near such locations, and much fine medicine was practiced. The Romans were particularly fond of hot springs; the town of Bath in England is named for its reputation as a spa, and the ancient Roman baths still function.

Because these hot springs often contained healing properties, and because they were of natural origin, it was widely believed that they were special gifts of God and signs of divine favor. As such, they were clearly under the protection of the spiritual beings who served God. Soon shrines or sanctuaries began to be erected near the springs, so that those who came could have a suitable place to ask God for healing, and to give thanks for cures and improvements in their condition.

Hot springs, although most dramatic in their appearance, were not the only sources of water with their own guardians. Natural wells and ordinary springs, even rivers and streams, were revered for their healing power; each had its guardian spirit. This belief prevailed in biblical times, too. Most people know the story of how Jacob came to the Jabbok River one night and there wrestled an angel until the breaking of the day. Those who study the folklore of religion say that the angel was the guardian of the river. Jewish tradition says it was Michael who wrestled with Jacob as a way of testing his worthiness to become a patriarch and the father of Israel. During the wrestling by the river, it says that Jacob's hip was put out of joint; Jewish tradition has always said it was Raphael who was sent by God to heal him.

By the time of Jesus, the Jews widely believed that Michael was the angel appointed by God to watch over certain sources of water, especially those with curative properties. This belief may stem from the fact that Michael is traditionally viewed as the special angel protector of the Jewish people, who would naturally associate his protective ministry with all the natural phenomena in their world.

But I think the association goes even deeper. Michael is traditionally viewed as the angel of the Exodus, who led the people of Israel through the waters of the Red Sea and who, when Moses struck the rock in the wilderness, brought forth the spring waters to quench the Israelites' thirst. In both these situations, the water involved brings life and safety to the Jews. So perhaps Michael's association with healing through water begins here.

An interesting passage in the gospel of John also relates to Michael's role in healing through water. John 5:5ff. reads: "Now in Jerusalem by the Sheep Gate is a pool called in Hebrew Bethesda, which has five porticoes.

In these lay many invalids, blind, lame, and paralyzed, waiting for the stirring of the waters; for an angel of the Lord went down at certain seasons into the pool and stirred up the water; whoever stepped in first after the stirring of the water was made well from whatever disease that person had."

Jewish tradition often associated the angel of the Lord who stirred up these waters with Michael (and the actual healing with Raphael).

Christian tradition followed Jewish tradition, and rededicated springs and healing waters, previously dedicated to pagan gods, to Michael the Archangel. One of the oldest of these is the sanctuary of St. Michael in Umbria, Italy, where the ancient spring once dedicated to Jupiter was renamed "to the God of angels" and placed under the protection of Michael as early as the fifth century.

In the time of the Emperor Justinian, sanctuaries of Michael were built throughout Asia Minor and Near Eastern European cities associated with healing waters. Perhaps the most famous were the healing springs of Bithynia, where there was also an attached hospital for the sick, both dedicated to Michael. On his traditional feast day, September 29, pilgrimages are still made to all of his shrines.

Today people still go to the many spas and hot springs all over the world in search of healing. "Taking the cure" is still a synonym for going to a spa to be treated for an ailment, and many different places throughout Europe specialize in treating different conditions and ailments through the drinking of the waters and special baths. In fact in many countries the health-care system actually pays for such therapies.

In Japan, where the traditional bath is still called a gift from God, healing hot springs are places of pilgrimage for millions of Japanese every year. In Shinto, the traditional religion of Japan, each spring is watched over by special guardian spirits called *kami*, whose presence and help are invoked by those who come for healing.

Why is Michael invoked for healing through water? My own understanding is that hot springs and other such places were seen as needing great protection, from both natural and supernatural disasters, on account of their immense value to humanity. Only the most powerful of protectors would possibly do for such important and holy places. For this reason, Michael was seen as the angel who must watch over places of healing. Such a notion still exists today in many places: for example, St. Michael's Medical Center in Newark, New Jersey, which was founded in 1867, is one of many hospitals dedicated to the archangel.

Michael is also viewed as the angel who helps lead the souls of the dying from this world into the next. He is the special patron of hospices, and when we are working with someone whose time in this world is ending, we can ask Michael to be with them on their journey to the other side.

# Michael and Raphael Working Together

My own experience is that Michael and Raphael work together to help us in our healing processes; it's not an either/or situation when angels are involved. When the need for healing is serious, as, for example, when someone is emotionally distraught following the death of a loved one, the protection of Michael is an important part of the healing process. The great archangel can, in a metaphorical sense, spread his wings around us to shield us from harmful influences that might prevent us from concentrating on our healing. In such a protective climate, our own guardian angels, working in harmony with Raphael, can help us heal.

We all have daily opportunities to ask our angels to help us heal our lives, but for people who work in the healing professions, the opportunities to have our angels work for healing are constant and enormous.

If I were a healer, I would put myself under the permanent aegis of Raphael and Michael. I would never enter a patient's room without quietly asking both my angel and the patient's angel for healing. I would never give a medication or a treatment without asking the angels involved to help make that treatment as effective as possible. In the evening, I would tell all my patients, "Sleep with the angels." In the morning, I would say to each, as the French farmers still do, "Good morning to you and to your companion"—meaning, of course, their angel.

I would call upon Raphael in particular when giving medicine or treatments, and I would speak to Michael, whose association particularly with water therapy is equally ancient.

And I would tell patients about their guardian angels, because it's very comforting to know that one's angel is never more than a heartbeat away. I have been a hospital patient four times in my life, and I can tell you, nights can be very long and lonely. Knowing my angel was at my bedside did much to get me through some very tough times. It's a good prescription for healing that more doctors ought to use: ℞: *Take two angels, and you may not need to call me in the morning.*

Those who are seriously ill, especially those in hospitals, often report seeing their angels or feeling their touch. Some caregivers laugh at this and say that it was just the pain medication speaking, but the patients know better. Their angels come to heal them, maybe not by restoring their bodies immediately, but by healing them of fear and anxiety, and giving them a sense of confidence and trust, and by raising their spirits; and sometimes, by telling them it's okay to let go. Sometimes they come to ease the person's transition from this world to the next.

And sometimes they even come to play. Martha Powers, whose story is in my first book, *Touched by Angels*, was hospitalized for a long time as a child, and she says that her angels came and played with her and kept her spirits up. Children are especially prone to actually seeing angels. Perhaps they are too young to know that seeing angels is "impossible," so they see them more easily. If I had a child in the hospital, I would want them to know that their angel is always with them, and that their parents' angels are, too. And I would have angel coloring books and read angel stories to them.

Angels want to help us heal. And the way we go about asking for such help is through prayer. But we must first explore our attitudes toward ourselves and those in our lives and see if, first of all, we need to ask or to grant forgiveness.

## Chapter Four

# Forgiveness—The Angelic Road to Personal Healing

> "Father, forgive them; they do not know what they are doing."
>
> —Matthew 28:30

he basis of all healing is forgiveness—the letting go, by conscious choice, of our hurt and anger at the wounds people and events have inflicted on us, and the injuries we have done to ourselves. Wherever there is a need for healing, there is a need for forgiveness. Forgiveness is the "angelic road" that leads to healing.

All of us, during the course of our lives in this world, are hurt by other people and hurt others. We do unloving things, we say hurtful words; or, conversely, we fail to say the loving thing when we should, or we see a need we could easily meet and turn away. And no matter what you call these events—illusion, karma, or sin—they cause wounds of spirit that can tear us apart, not just from each other, but from our very own souls.

75

This is a terrible situation. Here we are—we come from God, who is One, who is not only totally transcendent but perfectly immanent, oneness and unity permeating all creation, filled with knowing, creative love—and what is the first thing we do when we become aware of ourselves? We create disharmony, alienation, separation. What is even worse is that we accept this as a way of life. We get so used to being hurt and swallowing it, or hurting ourselves or others and then just moving on, that we don't even realize the depth of healing that we need. We become too wounded to care.

Our angels find this whole situation intolerable. They are perfect messengers, perfect communicators of God's love and grace. They don't sin or hurt any creature; there is no divisiveness in their society. All they want is for God's perfect love, harmony, and peace to dwell in us as these qualities are part of them. They hate seeing us cut off from ourselves and each other. They know it's unnatural.

For this reason, our angels are ready to work with us at all times so that we can forgive others and understand our own need to ask forgiveness where we have hurt others. Whenever we forgive or ask forgiveness, our angels are with us in a special and loving way. Jesus even said once: "There is joy in heaven among the angels whenever someone repents." I believe that's true. Our angels are filled with joy whenever we give up our spiritual blocks and blindness, whenever we tear down our personal Berlin Walls. I have personally felt the joy of my own angels, Enniss, Tallithia, and Kennisha, when I have asked forgiveness from God or from another, or when I have given my forgiveness to someone who has asked it.

Forgiveness and healing are inextricably linked. Forgiveness, whether we ask it or give it, is what begins the process that heals us of these terrible wounds. It's the most powerful spiritual medicine there is, because it stops the infection that wounds can cause, and lays the groundwork for love to grow in its place through reconciliation.

Forgiveness is not an emotion, a feeling of benevolence or compassion. It can be described as an act of will by which we decide to let go of a hurt. Deciding to forgive a hurt doesn't mean we condone or minimize it in the slightest. Rather, it means that we have decided not to retain the hurt and carry it in our heart and hold it against the individual who did the hurting. Being able to make such a decision is healing in itself, because it prevents a wound from being rubbed raw any further. And when forgiveness goes on to bloom in the peace of reconciliation, then love can enter and smooth away even the oldest and hardest of scar tissue. The trouble with most of us is that we are often so hurt that we decide we can live with scar tissue—we never work toward the kind of reconciliation that truly heals.

The best and easiest forgiveness comes when someone asks for forgiveness. But, because forgiveness is principally in our will and comes from our understanding, our knowledge, and our consciousness, we can forgive, even when the one who has hurt us will not or cannot ask for pardon.

Forgiveness is not always an instantaneous thing, of course. Sometimes it takes a long time to forgive. Sometimes it takes a lifetime. We have to grow in understanding and enlightenment before we can make a conscious decision to forgive, and often we have to reaffirm our decision many times before wounded feelings and emotions follow suit.

Sometimes forgiveness takes more than a lifetime. I personally believe that's what the Catholic notion of "Purgatory" is: a house of healing after we leave this world, a remedial school for the lessons we need to learn, that we should have learned while we were on earth.

# Healing in Progress

In December of 1992, I found myself on a national TV talk show. The day after it aired, which was about a week before Christmas, I was called into my boss's office and summarily fired from a job I had held for nearly five years. My work with angels was cited as a major factor in this decision. My boss produced a prepared envelope with a pink slip and told me I had fifteen minutes to clear out my desk. He had the corporate security personnel (who seemed very embarrassed at this) stand over me to make sure I didn't take any paper clips! It was a terrible experience, and I felt keenly the humiliation of it all. I went home and cried. I was so upset I doubt I could have heard the voice of God if it had come from a sonic boom just over my head. I was too hurt and sad and depressed. I was, as psychologists say, in mourning over my lost job.

And then, just after Christmas was over, the anger set in. I took stock of what little money I had, what I was likely to have from unemployment while I sought a new position, what small debts I had outstanding, and I started to do a slow boil.

*How dared they fire me!* I raged to myself. *I was the best managing editor they ever had. I carried a workload that would have felled another person. I was good at my job. My boss really had it in for me. He really enjoyed firing me. He wanted to hire someone else, not someone who had been there before he was hired, etc. . . .* I ranted on and on in my mind, imagining all sorts of things. I relived the humiliating nightmare of following the security people down the long corridor and out to the parking garage. I shivered, I cried, I hated. I invented ways of getting back at the company. I debated naming names. I thought about going to a lawyer. I was paralyzed with anger—and paralysis of the spirit can be even more debilitating than physical paralysis. My ego was in shreds.

It was awful, one of the worst experiences of my life. I am a devout pacifist by nature, as is my whole family. The last close relative I had who went to war fought in the American Revolution. My father was a conscientious objector in World War II. I had always been raised to believe that peace in the world starts with peace in each heart, and here I was hating my boss with a hatred that grew daily, and hating myself for hating.

Because of the anger and hate that had seized my soul and were fighting for possession, I found my entire spiritual life blocked. Every time I prayed to God, I would be distracted by vindictive thoughts. I would talk to Enniss for hours on end, and he was silent. (Obviously, it was the cacophony in my soul and the enthusiastic efforts of dark spirits that were blocking his words. *He* never stopped trying to communicate.) My battered and bruised ego was firmly in the way. I was totally absorbed in myself.

My life came to a total standstill. I couldn't write

anything worth reading for *AngelWatch*™, the magazine about angels that I publish. I didn't have the heart to give talks about angels, because all I could think about was my anger. I relived the event over and over in my mind, and each time I did I found new details to make me sick at heart. Every time I went to Mass, I felt guilty. After all, I was there to celebrate the universal forgiveness of God through the person of Jesus, and I couldn't break out of myself to join in. In the middle of the Christmas Midnight Mass, I was so angry at my former boss that when I mentally said, "Damn it," I realized I was close to meaning it literally. The thought that a part of me could actually almost wish someone an eternity away from the love of God was so terrifying that I spent most of the Christmas Midnight Mass shivering and crying.

Added to this, I had a book to write—I had just signed the contract with Warner Books to write *Touched by Angels*. But I was so wounded from what had happened (and frankly, from what I was doing to myself) that for nearly three weeks I just sat at my computer and got nowhere. I was too filled with anger to write about God and the angels.

And so, since I was in no mood to listen to God's words via my angel, Enniss inspired all of my friends and family to talk to me and help me to release my anger by forgiving those who had fired me. It seemed that, no matter whom I talked to about being fired, they would answer, "Really, Eileen, don't you see it's part of the plan? You weren't supposed to be working for that company anymore. That's all. God has something else in mind. Let go of it."

No matter how gloomy I got, everyone said the same thing, even friends who, to my certain knowledge, had never talked about God or angels or faith before. At the time, it struck me as eerie. No matter what I said about how injured or wounded I was, how unjust the company, they all said the same thing: "Don't worry; it's part of the plan." It was as though, for three weeks, I had the same conversation with fifteen or twenty different people. I could have written the script for the Bill Murray movie *Groundhog Day*, about the guy who had to live the same day over and over until he learned a lesson about life.

In retrospect, the whole episode seems kind of funny. I can laugh now, because as much as can be healed in this world has been healed. It *was* part of the plan that my old job end so something more wonderful could begin. I will never be able to thank Enniss enough for all his efforts to keep me connected to God's reality and to get me out of the wounded ego trip I was on.

Finally, after dozens of friends had told me the truth, I was able to think rationally again, and it began to sink in that I should not only forgive the company that had fired me, but I should also give thanks for losing my old job, rather than harbor resentment and anger. When I had calmed down enough to see and feel the depth of the wound inside me, I began to ask for healing, and to try to forgive. I kept thinking of Jesus, who is my model for the perfect life, dying in agony on a Roman cross, with nails tearing at his flesh and nerves, yet still able to say, "Father, forgive them; they don't understand what they are doing."

Slowly, as I asked God to send the angels of healing and enlightenment to help me, I began to see that my former employer was simply acting out of their fear of the unknown. The fact is, they are an honorable company overall, and they bend over backwards to deal fairly with their clients, one of whom is still me. I realized that I had my own faults, and that they contributed to the whole business as well. Our interests had diverged.

I also was able to separate out the different strands associated with the event. I hadn't been able to see that there was nothing wrong with one job ending in order for another to begin—it happens all the time. It was not necessary to forgive the company for ending my employment. It was, in fact, their choice. What was wrong about the whole scenario in my mind was the *way* I had been fired—with anger and total unconcern for me. And so I stood in the middle of my kitchen one day, with clenched fists and a jaw that ached from resentment, and a chronic headache from being a prisoner of ego, and I unclenched my fists and said, "I, Eileen Elias Freeman, hereby forgive ———— for firing me."

Did something miraculous happen? Was I washed with relief, bathed in joy and release? No, not at all. In fact, I scarcely felt any different. Two minutes later I was still reliving the humiliation and resentment. But as soon as I realized what was happening, I unclenched my fists again and said quietly, "No, that is not right. I forgive them for firing me. I choose to let it go." I probably said it a hundred times a day for weeks. But what was important was that I had, with the grace of God, begun the healing process.

When I was finally able to begin the forgiving process, I found that I could write again. The angels helped me make up for lost time, and the manuscript was finished on schedule. But I would never have been able to write a single word if the process of forgiveness had not been begun.

The forgiveness/healing process went on for several months with my affirming my forgiveness for being fired. And I truly had begun to believe that I had forgiven them—in my mind. But my feelings were still badly hurt, my emotions were still raw.

One day I was talking on the phone to the artist K. Martin-Kuri, whose organization Tapestry has sponsored several angel conferences. She asked me if I would speak on the subject of forgiveness at the Second American Angel Conference in June of 1993.

I gulped. I could talk on the *theory* of forgiveness, and explain how I ask my angels to come and help me with the enlightenment I need to forgive those who have hurt me. But how could I claim any credibility, when I was still not healed inside from what had happened to me? I said that I would be glad to give the talk if I could subtitle my words "A Work in Progress." She agreed.

From then on I began to spend time in meditation specifically working to heal my feelings and to cement the forgiveness I had given to my former boss. It took time, especially because a reconciliation, which is always the fastest avenue of healing, wasn't possible.

Whenever the hurt came back to haunt me, instead of letting the knife twist in the wound, I imagined myself, my ex-boss, Jesus, and our guardian angels all sitting together, trying to talk things out with love instead of fear and anger. At first it was difficult. My mind would back off and I would cringe mentally at the hurt memories; then I would have to re-enter the conference room I had created in my mind and plug back into the inner conversation. (Later on in the process I learned to create a neutral, healing environment, rather than one associated with the hurt.)

By the time I gave the talk at the conference I had reached a point where I could at least shake hands with my supervisor's guardian angel, if not with my boss. And later I could visualize Jesus hugging both my boss and me. I believe that in the next world, if not in this, my ex-boss and I will come together in the light of God and finally be healed of whatever wounds remain.

# Living in Forgiveness

If we accept the fact that we are the children of God, then we must commit ourselves totally to living a life in love that is worthy of the One who created us. Not only must we strive to be at peace with ourselves and others, but we must work conscientiously at forgiving all who have hurt us, offended us, sinned against us. We cannot make compromises with deadly wounds. We do not have the misguided liberty to say, "I think I can live with *this* wound and *that* hurt." We must work to heal them all. We were meant to be whole.

This means that when we do something unloving, something that hurts someone else, we must ask for their forgiveness. It doesn't matter what our intention was; if we hurt someone, even unintentionally, we need to ask for forgiveness.

And we must seek equally to forgive all those who have ever hurt us, whether they ask for forgiveness or not. We will never be healed ourselves if we do not reach out to help others heal. St. Peter once asked Jesus how often he should forgive someone—up to seven times? Jesus answered, "Not seven times, but seventy times seven," meaning, without limit. He said also, "If someone sins against you seven times a day, and seven times a day asks you to forgive, you must forgive."

If someone hurts you, they may be touched by grace to understand what they did or failed to do was unloving. They may come to you and say, "I'm sorry for what I did. Can you ever forgive me?" When this happens, don't make the mistake of saying, "Oh, that's all right. These things happen. Just forget it." The person has come to you for forgiveness, not dismissal, for healing, not a bandage. The most important thing to say is, "Yes, I forgive you."

Remember, forgiveness at its heart is an act of will, of choice. Your feelings may still be deeply hurt, and there may be other wounds in need of healing, but you *can* choose to forgive. If the wound was so terrible that you're not ready, at least acknowledge it and ask for help from God, and from your angels, especially Raphael, who is the angel of healing par excellence. Keep it in the forefront of your consciousness, for it is a wound, and if you ignore it, it may become infected and poison your soul.

And when you are the one asking for forgiveness, don't take a "that's okay" for an answer. Ask, "But do you *forgive* me?" If the one you have hurt forgives you, then reconciliation and healing of memories will be possible much sooner and much more completely. I find that in these situations it often helps for me to speak to the other person's guardian angel in advance. I ask the angel to help the person know that I am coming to ask forgiveness for something. And when someone has hurt me, I ask their angels to show them I've been hurt, so they will ask for forgiveness.

# Forgiving Each Other

As all of us know from personal experience, it sometimes happens that we can't bring ourselves to forgive someone who has wounded us deeply, even when they come and ask for forgiveness. A few weeks after I returned from the second American Angel Conference in June of 1993, a close friend—I'll call her Annaliese—called me to ask me whether she could get her husband's angel "fired." She was very angry and hurt, because she had just found out that her husband—I'll call him Pak—had had a brief affair with a co-worker. "He doesn't deserve a guardian angel anymore," she said.

I was surprised, because her husband had never struck me as the sort of person to be unfaithful, but I had to tell her that no, she couldn't get her husband's angel fired, because she hadn't "hired" him in the first place. What she needed was for her husband to ask her forgiveness and for her to be able to grant that forgiveness, so reconciliation and healing could take place. (Obviously, their relationship needed far more healing than just that, but reconciliation would at least be a start.) It appeared as we talked that until this incident happened, she was basically satisfied with the quality of their marriage.

"I'll never forgive him!" she cried. "What he did was unforgivable!" She went on in this vein for some time. Clearly, she was terribly wounded.

"What did he say about it?" I asked.

"He said he just got drunk at the Fourth of July office picnic and forgot about where he was, and that it was over and would never happen again."

"And what did you say?"

"I told him I wanted him to get out." She went on and on for some minutes before I stopped her.

"It seems to me that neither of you is getting to the heart of the matter. Your husband hasn't actually asked for forgiveness, and so you haven't been forced into deciding whether or not you want to forgive him. And you have let pride and wounded vanity make the whole question worse. Both of you are dancing around the problem, and even if you somehow stay together, you'll never heal." I knew the wound would scar over, and scar tissue is not normal tissue.

Crying, she asked me for help. "Can you get your angels to do something?"

"Why don't *you* ask *your* angels for help?" I asked her to do three things: first, to pray to God for openness and to let go of her wounded vanity, which was caused by her husband's cheating on her; second, to ask her angel to teach her about forgiving her husband; third, to ask her husband's angel to urge him to ask forgiveness. She agreed to do this daily for a week and to call me back.

I was surprised two days later to get a call from Pak, to whom she had related our conversation. "She just won't listen to me," he said ruefully. "I've tried to apologize, I brought her flowers, but she just turns me off."

"Have you clearly asked her to forgive you for hurting her so deeply in breaking your marriage vows?"

"I said I was really sorry."

I explained that saying one is sorry is simply a personal statement; it doesn't reach out to acknowledge the other person's hurt and try to heal it.

"What can I do? She won't listen to anything I say now. She won't speak to me."

It seemed clear that Pak was as deeply enmeshed in feelings of worthlessness as Annaliese was in wounded ego. I suggested that for the next week he, too, should do three things; first, tell God how sorry he was for the tremendous hurt he had caused his wife; second, ask her angel to tell her how sorry he was for hurting her; third, ask his wife directly to forgive him for his infidelity.

About a week later, Pak called me. "I've been doing what you suggested. Every time I pass her, I say, 'Honey, I'm so sorry for hurting you. Please, I'm begging you to forgive me.' She keeps saying she can't."

"At least she's talking to you," I pointed out. "Forgiveness begins with communication." I told him to keep on asking his angel for help in communicating his hope to be forgiven.

A few days later the wife called me. "We both wondered if you might be willing to come over for dinner and talk to us," she asked. "We think we need someone to help arbitrate."

I felt a bit awkward, because I have no training whatsoever in counseling, but I listened for what God might say in my heart, and I felt I should go, just as a friend, and trust in grace to know what to say.

When I was praying later that day for enlightenment,

I remembered a verse in the book of Job, which spoke of Job's wish for an angel to act as his arbiter before God (Job 33:23). I asked God for special insight to hear what my own angel arbiter might share with me that night about this couple's need. And I began to see in my mind how I might be able to help.

When I arrived at the house, I suggested that we sit down together before we had dinner. It was an awkward situation. Neither Annaliese nor Pak would even sit with each other.

I explained that, rather than talk things out, I would like to pray with them and then lead all three of us in a guided meditation. They agreed. I could see that both of them wanted forgiveness and healing, but one was too hurt to grant it, and the other was too depressed to ask it anymore.

I began with praying out loud, entrusting the three of us to the love of God through the ministry of our angels. I asked in faith for what I believed was necessary: the asking for forgiveness and the granting of the same.

Then I had Annaliese and Pak do some breathing and relaxation exercises, and when it seemed right, I began a guided meditation. In brief, I said: "The two of you are sitting on a bench at Echo Lake [a local park]. It is early morning; no one is around but yourselves. You are surrounded by a beautiful blue light, which is symbolic of God's loving presence. Standing in front of you are your own guardian angels." And I had them visualize those heavenly messengers who watch over them.

"First of all, I want each of you to pray to God, from whom all love and forgiveness come. The darkness has been working on both of you, and as a result you've

89

become so enmeshed in feelings of guilt or hopelessness or hatred that the healing voice of God has been drowned in a sea of emotion.

"Now you're going to ask your own guardian angel for help. Pak, you need to own up to how much you've hurt your wife, so you can ask her to forgive you. Annaliese, you need to ask for help to give up the resentment and pain you're clinging to."

When they had done this, I said, "Now, Annaliese, I want you to talk to Pak's guardian angel, and ask him to help Pak ask forgiveness. And Pak, you talk to Annaliese's angel and ask her to help clear the resentment out of her heart so she will forgive."

Both Pak and Annaliese followed my suggestions with great sincerity and purpose, and I knew that God, through the angels, was working in their hearts. But I also sensed that the fallen angels, whose perverse delight is in fostering separation and divisiveness, would not give up without a struggle. I explained quietly that they would have to call upon Michael the great Prince of Hosts to "do battle," so to speak, with the dark angels. I had them visualize the dark angels (reassuring them that the light of God was protecting them) being soundly defeated by Michael and his angels of light. They told me afterwards that they could both see a fierce battle, as it were, going on all around them in the park. I told them that for this to be successful, they would have to give up, with all their strength of will, all of the evil in their lives that had to do with the issue at hand.

Annaliese suddenly got up, anger written all over her face, and began walking away rapidly toward the kitchen. I would have followed, but Pak began to sob and to cry in Korean (his first language). Clearly God's grace had broken into his heart and he was not only free of the dark influences but was seeing what he had done to his wife clearly for the first time.

I went out to the kitchen, where Annaliese, too, was crying. Hearing her husband had touched her heart. I led her back into the living room, and I was glad to see that she, without thinking about it, sat down next to Pak.

It took some time for both to quiet down, each absorbed in their own thoughts. When they were calm again, I said, "Michael has driven away the dark angels by the power of God. Pak, don't you have something to ask of your wife?"

I waited, hoping that he would speak. And he did. Breaking into tears once more, he cried, "Annaliese, I'm so sorry for hurting you. I love you. I was so wrong." And while I listened, he finished with the necessary words, "Can you ever forgive me?" And his sincerity was evident.

Annaliese put her arms around him and cried. She was more hesitant than he, and I knew her feelings were still terribly wounded, but she replied, "Yes, Pak, I do forgive you. I love you, too." And they looked directly at each other for the first time since I had come.

I told them that we would finish our meditation. "The park is now filled with angels and they are all dancing with joy because of you two. They include the angels of all the people you work with and know, because now all that dark energy in your lives is gone and can't affect the people they are guardian angels to, the people you meet every day at work and in the stores. The light around you is growing lighter and brighter, turning from protective blue to radiant gold and white.

"Take a moment to thank God for the enlightenment that has helped the both of you break through this wall of separation. Now call upon Raphael, the Healer of God, and ask him to take your need for healing and lay it within God's heart. And visualize Jesus sending his healing love upon you. Believe that healing for your hurt feelings will come, Annaliese. Trust that healing for your feelings of worthlessness will grow, Pak."

I went on to remind them to forgive themselves, too, and to ask God for forgiveness.

And finally, I had them imagine that the circle of dancing angels had swept them up into the dance, and that the steps circled and swirled to heaven.

It took some time for the three of us to ease back from the experience. It had been one of the most intense things I had shared for a very long time, but Pak and Annaliese were so desperate to be out of a situation that both hated that they really gave it all their energy.

We never even thought about dinner that evening. Instead we talked until after midnight about ways to continue the healing process. I reminded Annaliese that she would have to affirm her forgiveness for some time, until her own hurt feelings and emotions were healed. They decided to see a counselor, too.

Over the next few months Pak and Annaliese worked to heal their relationship through forgiveness. There were no bright lights from heaven, no angelic appearances, no miracles. But both Annaliese and her husband told me many times that they felt the presence, not only of their guardian angels, but also of another angel they called the "angel of their marriage." The hardest part, they said, was healing the wounded emotions and memories. Annaliese kept dreaming of the moment when she had found out about her husband's infidelity (through a well-meaning, but anonymous letter). Pak said he kicked himself around the block every time he relived the moment when Annaliese showed him the letter, and, with tears in her eyes, asked him if it was true.

I showed them how to revisualize the scene in a way that could lead to healing of memories. For Annaliese, I explained that every time the memories came back, she should imagine herself holding the unopened letter and having a conversation with her guardian angel, visualizing the angel putting her arms around Annaliese and telling her that she was there for her and would help support her. I asked Pak to do the same, and to imagine his angel telling him how much he still loved him, how much God still loved him.

I also suggested that they try to be angels to each other, to do small, loving things for each other without thought of reward. In this way they would not only build up a treasure trove of positive memories, but they would come to understand better the sorts of things that our angels do for us from behind the scenes to help us heal and grow.

As I write this, they're still working on the healing of memories, and with the grace of God and the help of their angels, they are succeeding.

# Divine Forgiveness

Forgiveness is not a two-way street between individuals. God is also involved. We must also ask God's forgiveness when we have hurt someone, or ourselves or even the environment. God is the One who has put such beautiful and perfect order into the world. Whenever we detract from that harmony by creating division, by stepping out of the plan, it is right and necessary to ask God to forgive us, and not only to forgive us, but to increase our enlightenment and understanding so we can grow, in addition to being healed and restoring the balance we have disrupted. And God, who is perfect understanding, and whose compassion for us is sure, will always forgive, and pour out upon us the wisdom and grace we need for our lives.

God's angels are often the mediators of such gifts; they bring them to us and try to help us use them well. Our angels live in God's love and light in a way we do not, at least not while we are in this world. Everything they do is totally in conformity with the divine plan. They do not have their own agendas. But because forgiveness and healing are always part of the plan, angels are always looking for ways to help us forgive and be forgiven.

## Forgiving Ourselves

Sometimes our greatest obstacle to healing is our inability to forgive ourselves for our faults, even when our faith tells us God has forgiven us, and any others involved have offered their forgiveness as well. This was true in Pak's situation. He's still occasionally kicking himself around the block, beating himself up inside, although

Annaliese has truly forgiven him and has never brought up his affair again.

When we can't forgive ourselves, I think it's most often a matter of our egos—either too much or too little. Sometimes we think so little of ourselves that we just cannot make ourselves believe that we deserve forgiveness for something we have done or failed to do. We can't even trust that the other person really forgives us. We say we accept their forgiveness, but deep inside we're saying, "If s/he only knew how rotten I really am, they'd never forgive me." We just don't love ourselves or see ourselves as deserving of love.

I went through such negative thoughts for years. I did not grow up with any of the physical attractions that made other girls and women my age popular, and the skills and abilities I had were not much appreciated by my peers. I came to believe that if anything went wrong, it was my fault, and it was my fault that it *was* my fault.

For me, it was my faith in God's love in sending Jesus into the world that changed me. Like many people, I had seen the side of religion that viewed God as a patriarch sitting on a throne and ready to punish people harshly for the slightest infractions, and I rejected it. But when I came to see that in Jesus there was a perfect mirror of the divine love, I realized how lovable I am, and I was able to separate out the bad things I might do from the fact that I was not a bad person.

If you have feelings of low self-esteem, as I did, it can hinder your healing. It is often helpful to develop a personal, outward-directed affirmation and to use it as often as you can. For example: *Dear and loving God, I believe you love me, and therefore I love myself.*

I am also fond of the verse from the deuterocanonical book of Wisdom: "You love all things that exist, God, and hate none of the things you have made; for you would not have made anything in the first place if you had hated it, O Lover of all."

Our angels are very willing partners in helping us realize how loved we are. They love us with all the love they have, and that is a great deal of love. I often suggest to people that they visualize their angel standing behind them and encircling them with its love, in the shape of a pink light. (There's nothing magical about the color pink. It's simply a color that most people associate with affection.) If you want to humanize your angel by making it a he or she, or by giving him wings or dressing her in a beautiful gown, go ahead.

Then, think of the things that make you cringe inside the most, and feel the angel's arms tightening even more around you. Visualize the light becoming deeper and brighter, until it becomes red and warm. Hear your angels tell you they love you.

Of course, sometimes our egos become the opposite: so inflated that we just can't believe we did something for which we need to ask forgiveness. We forget we're human and fallible. We can't forgive ourselves because we've made ourselves into a vengeful God with no compassion for weakness. This is what happened to Pak. He is a real perfectionist, obsessive in his drive to be right at all times.

Changing our view of God from a judge to a lover is a difficult process, but it can be done, if one wants to. How to do it is beyond the scope of this book, but I know that our angels will support us in all our efforts. And when we no longer see God as ready to punish us, then our hearts will be ruled by love and compassion for ourselves, and we can give up the masochistic need to punish ourselves forever.

The process of forgiveness can be slow and complex. But forgiveness, at its heart, is simple. It's the way we restore harmony in our lives, in the lives of those around us, and in the cosmos, when that harmony has been disrupted by sin, hurt, and malice. If we only acknowledge our need to forgive and be forgiven, ask God for help to understand, and work with our angels to put things right in our lives, we will be healed, and the world with us.

# Chapter Five
# Praying with Our Angels for Healing

> Then, if there should be an angel, a mediator, one
> of a thousand, one who declares a person upright,
> who is gracious to the person . . . who prays for
> that individual . . .
>
> —Job 33:23, 26

f forgiveness is often the basis of healing, then prayer is its fuel. *Prayer* is speaking to God with words, whether aloud or silently, conversing with the loving Source of all we are and have. And because God is conscious, aware, purposeful, caring, and not some deaf celestial clockmaker, God speaks in reply to our prayers.

*Meditation*, insofar as it is related to prayer, is the process by which we try to free our minds of words and concepts, so that we can listen with all of our attention to what God says to us, either directly or through our angels. Some kinds of meditation, particularly those designed to help us focus on our needs, are deliberately self-centered, and this is not necessarily bad; but the meditation side of prayer aims at *kenosis*, the emptying of the ego, in order to be filled with God's presence.

*Contemplation* is active, God-directed prayer without any words or even mental concepts or images, like direct current in contrast to alternating current. Contemplation, like God's reply or like the visit of an angel, is a gift independent of our efforts, although we can and should practice the kinds of God-seeking that leave us open to such moments.

Prayer is as simple as any other kind of speech. The difficulty for us humans is that the other party in our conversation, God, is normally not visible or perceptible to our senses, and there is nothing we can do to change that. God manifests the divine presence in ways and at times that we cannot control. As a result, we often stop praying, because God doesn't respond when or how we expect.

This is a serious mistake. We have a basic need to seek God; it's inherent, it's as necessary to us as breathing and eating. Blaise Pascal, the French philosopher, once said that there is a God-shaped vacuum in the center of every human soul, and that we are driven to fill it up. Saint Augustine said, long before Pascal, "Our hearts are restless, O God, and they cannot rest until they rest in You."

Every people, every society, every culture, seeks God in whatever ways it knows how. The earliest human literature from ancient Sumeria is about God. Stone Age burials from Neanderthal times already show evidence of a belief in a world beyond our own.

The problem occurs when a society forgets its spiritual purpose. For too long, we have worshiped an unholy trinity called Money, Power, and Prestige. And we have become steadily impoverished, robbed of power, and humiliated as a result. Why? Because what we have given our souls to is no god at all, and our immortal spirit, our soul, cannot be nourished except by God. We need to recover our priorities if we want to heal our lives. Our angels know this, because their priorities are as they should be: God before all, and everything in God.

We live on this planet for a short time, and we must do the very best with the talents and gifts we have, but our destiny is not for this world. When we shed our space suits, that is, our bodies, our immortal spirits enter an eternal realm where our perceptions of God are heightened beyond anything we can even conceive of here on earth, a realm where we can grow and develop and evolve forever within the love and wisdom of God. And the way we orient ourselves toward God in this world—as preparation for our eternal future—is through prayer.

All conscious creation prays or speaks to God. The angels pray to God, just as we do, but because they are spirits and are not weighed down with space suits, their prayer is one of contemplation, unconcerned with words or concepts as we know them.

Prayer is at the heart of every angel's being. Long before there was an earth to protect or humans to be guardians of, the angels existed to reflect joyously back to God the glory of the divine. In Job 38:4, 7, God asks Job, "Where were you when I laid the cornerstone of the earth, when the morning stars sang together, and all the heavenly beings shouted for joy?"

We pray, alone or with others, for many reasons. Most of our reasons have angelic counterparts. The more we can pray not only *with* the angels but *like* the angels, the more we understand who we really are and the better we can heal our lives, because we will be in closer contact with the One who is our healer.

There are five basic forms of prayer: adoration, praise, thanksgiving, petition, and repentance. If those terms sound scary, then think of them as: loving, admiring, thanking, asking, and saying I'm sorry.

# Adoration

The most basic form of prayer is adoration. When we pray in this way, our prayer is most like that of the angels.

Adoration is acknowledging and extolling the basic loving relationship between us and God. It is understanding that God is God and that we are most assuredly not God. Adoration is a healing prayer, because it establishes a right relationship between ourselves and the Creator of all; it puts who we are and who God is in their proper perspectives. It helps us place our footsteps firmly onto the path of reality. Adoration opens our eyes so we can see ourselves as we really are. It fills us with light so that anything that is darkness in us can be revealed and healed.

The angels' most basic prayer is one of adoration. Every religion makes this clear. Isaiah's vision of God included the sight of seraphim, heavenly beings who cried out, "Holy, holy, holy is the Lord of Hosts!" (Isaiah 6:2). John's vision of the same sight of God included the sight of "myriads of myriads and thousand of thousands" of angels who fell on their faces before the One seated on the throne and "worshiped the One who lives forever and ever."

In some ways adoration is the hardest prayer for us,

because it requires that we put our egos totally aside and contemplate only the worthiness of the divine. (The very word *worship* means "worth-ship," i.e., acknowledging the worthiness of God.) We need to get out of the selfish mode that says each of us is the center of the universe and see with the poet T. S. Eliot that God the Word is the "still point of the turning world."

# Praise

Praise is the second kind of prayer for both humans and angels. Praise is only possible when we have come to the point of first adoring God, of establishing an appropriate understanding of who we are in relation to God. Praise is acknowledging the wonderful qualities of God, like love, wisdom, compassion, power, etc.

Angels praise God because their beings are full of appreciation and love for the divine plan. They see with great clarity much more of God's purpose in creating the world and in giving us—we humans and the angels—unending life and consciousness.

Praise can be healing for us, since it draws us out of ourselves and reduces our egoism. When we give praise to God, obviously we are confessing all of those good and beautiful qualities that are part of the divine. Just speaking about love, beauty, clarity, peace, patience, knowledge, and other things raises our spirits. Further, it draws our attention away from ourselves; it tends outward. But the spiritual energy that we sense when we touch God in this way is a positive force in our lives. It is one reason why our angels draw us into prayer. They know that prayer is energizing, and that that kind of energy is healing.

Praise, like adoration, is a kind of prayer that our angels will always join with us in offering to God. One of the last counsels Raphael offered to Tobias and his family was: "Bless God each and every day; sing his praises." (12:18). The psalms, those beautiful and universal prayers, even call upon the angels to laud the Almighty: Psalm 148 sings, "Praise the Lord, you his angels; praise him all his host."

# Blessing and Thanksgiving

Prayer of thanksgiving is the first kind of prayer that partly includes ourselves. Praise and adoration are totally fixed on God. We scarcely enter into the picture. With thanksgiving, we are speaking to God in relation to ourselves. We acknowledge God's loving grace and working in our lives. We are grateful for love, concern, help, enlightenment, deliverance, peace, and so much more.

I subtitled this section "Blessing and Thanksgiving" because blessing is a bit different from thanksgiving. Blessing is a kind of mixture of praise and thanksgiving. It's thanksgiving without speaking in terms of something human to be thankful *for*. Or one might see it as thanking God, not for something *we* have received, but for the wonder, love, and beauty of our Source.

I believe that our ability and willingness to speak to God in the prayer of thanksgiving are a barometer of how much healing has been accomplished already in our lives. After all, healing, whether of physical ills or wounds of the spirit, is something to give thanks to God for. If we can't recall having thanked God for healing our lives, then perhaps we need to work on our healing more intensely.

Angels, too, voice their thanksgiving to God. I hope that doesn't seem strange to you. Angels are creatures, as we are, dependent as totally upon the same Source for their lives and their growth as we are. They give thanks for many of the same things: life, love, purpose, faculties of comprehension and appreciation, the ability to grow. They bless God for the divine plan, so filled with wisdom and magnificence.

Our angels join their prayer with ours whenever we thank God. But because thanksgiving is partly an "us"-centered prayer, our prayers of thanksgiving and those of the angels will diverge. When we say, "O God, I bless you for the beauties of the world," our angels join in without a single difference (although their knowledge and appreciation of the beauties of the world will be far more complete than ours are). But when we pray, "O God, I thank you for helping me get through losing my job last year," our angels are going to be praying in a parallel way, not in the same words. After all, they didn't lose their jobs last year. They may say, "O God, I thank you for showing me how to help Eileen best learn the wonderful things you have in store for her because of gaining a new job. I thank you for letting me minister to her your unsearchable healing love."

So our angels will join in with us gladly whenever we speak to God of our thanks for all we have received, but they may more often join in the spirit of our prayer than in the actual sentiments.

Thanksgiving is a very human, very basic sort of thing. We even have a national celebration, a day whose purpose is to give thanks. In any language, one of the most quickly learned phrases is "thank you." So it shouldn't be difficult for us to use the phrase to God.

We can also say thank you to our angels, just as we would thank a human friend for their help, but we say it on a very different level than we do to God. For example, it would not have been appropriate for me to thank Enniss for helping me forgive my ex-boss for firing me. Enniss didn't do that for me; it was the grace of God, a loving Parent giving me enlightenment, that enabled me to do that. When I was able to forgive, I thanked God for the gift, for the wisdom, for the insights. But on another level I thanked Enniss, too, because without his counsel, his advice, his quiet whisperings in my soul, I might well have missed God's healing grace. I might have clung to resentment and not opened my soul to peace.

All of us have grown up with the notion of counting our blessings in times of trouble. Just numbering our blessings, however, only keeps us centered in our own egos, and we learn nothing. It's when we thank the Source of all blessings, when we go outside our own egos, that we can grow whole, that we can heal. After all, we're not misers or people for whom life is a matter of quantity rather than quality.

One of the healing things I believe our angels do for us all the time is to remind us how blessed each of us is.

Our heavenly guardians are always telling us of the good things, the whole things, that are part of us. They work to counteract the negativity all around us, sometimes even in our own hearts. The fact is that there *are* fallen angels, poor, sad beings whose whole lives are lived in darkness, sick with a terminal illness of their fundamental spirit, and their very presence can infect us with their depressing, evil, destructive miasma unless we listen to our angels instead, who only want our health.

# Asking God: Petition and Intercession

There are two forms of addressing our requests to God: petition and intercession. Petition comes from the Latin word meaning "request." When we ask God for "things," whether small or great, we are petitioning.

Intercession is praying to God on behalf of another person, holding them in our arms and lifting them to God. It's a very energizing, and often draining, form of prayer. In fact, the very meaning of the word implies being right in the middle of things. It's far more other-oriented than mere petition. Both have their place in our lives.

Our requests to God run the gamut of everything we can comprehend. And it's right for us to ask God for whatever we need and want. Doing so can be healing to our often inflated egos, because it forces us in a gentle way to remember that we are not God, that all we are and have comes from God. Of course we have to develop the proper attitude when we pray for something or for someone. God is not a fairy godmother who turns pumpkins into coaches at our request. We can't make demands on God, or treat God like a divination tool. There's no magic formula for making God agree to what we would like to have happen. God is God, that is to say, totally sovereign.

But given that this is so, it is also true that God knows everything, including our needs, even before we ask. The biblical psalmist once said, "O God, you have searched me and you know me. You know when I go out and when I go in. . . . Before a word is on my tongue, you know it already." Because God knows everything, God is not capricious. God will always grant our needs.

God will not, however, always grant our *wants*. So if we ask for something we feel we need, and we don't receive it, it surely means that either it wasn't a need in the first place, or that it is a need, but not now.

Intercessory prayer is less self-centered than other kinds of petition, because the object of our prayers is not ourselves but someone else. When we pray for someone's good, because of our love for them, then many unseen wounds of spirit are healed within us, even without our knowing it. I have always felt that when we intercede for others, there is a special energy of healing that rests upon us as well. Going out of our egos to feel another's need and offer it to God helps restore the balance of creation.

Of course we can always be hit by the "ego through the back door" trick, where we think we're praying out of sheer goodwill for someone, let's say, to stop smoking. Suddenly we realize that we're not so much concerned for the other person's healing; rather, we just want to stop the drain on the household budget that cigarettes cause, or the smell of smoke that we can't get out of the rug.

Thank God for our angels' prayers for us! Angels' prayers of asking and petition are fundamentally different from ours. For one thing, they don't ask for things for themselves. Petition, per se, is not a quality of angelic prayer. They are totally centered in the divine; for that reason they have perfect confidence that they already have whatever they need. The things we pray most often about—life, health, finances, etc.—are personally meaningless to angels. Their life is eternal, health is not an issue, and money is totally irrelevant.

Angels act as intercessors for us all the time. Of course God's loving care is not dependent on whether we have powerful patrons in high places! But as intercessors, angels have no peer in the realm of the created universe. Our guardian angels are always interceding, putting themselves right in the middle on our behalf. The biblical Job, whose concern was to have his angel act as an intercessor with a God whose actions he could not understand, said to his friends, "Even now my witness is in heaven, and he who vouches for me is on high, the interpreter of my thoughts to God, unto Whom my eye drips." (As translated by Marvin Pope, *Job*, New York: Doubleday, 1973.) We, too, have angels who act as intercessors, always speaking of us before the face of God.

# Repentance

*Repentance* is an old-fashioned word, but then again, so is *angel*, so is *human*. It refers to the way we acknowledge before God things we have done that are not a part of the divine plan. It also includes our realizing that we have left undone good things that we should have accomplished. Repentance means that we see the evil in our lives and turn away from it—and tell God so. When our prayer is a prayer of repentance, we accept the responsibility for evil we have done or good we have failed to do, and we tell God we are sorry and hope to do better. Repentance is a necessary part of our prayer, because not one of us is perfect.

Repentance is the one form of prayer that angels do not know how to pray. Not a single angel who serves God needs to repent of anything, because all of them live in perfect harmony with God's plan for creation.

The prayer of repentance is not a matter of craven fear in the sight of God, like a fearful child who has broken the cookie jar. It is not wounded ego kicking us around the block, saying, "How could I have been so stupid as to drink and drive?" Rather, it is the loving trust of a child in the parent, even when the child has done something the parent has said not to do. There is no fear of punishment in repentance, only faith in the God who heals. If we want to heal our lives, we must learn to accept the responsibility for the evil we do and the good we leave undone.

If you still see God as the patriarchal hurler of thunderbolts who spies on your every fault in order to exact every bit of punishment, then I suggest you ask your angel to help you pray in a more confident fashion. The apostle John, who walked with Jesus, and who had one of the most extraordinary out-of-body experiences in history, observed, "There is no fear in love, but perfect love casts out fear."

In working with the angels of God, I have learned to

believe this: we never pray alone. It may be late at night, and we may feel as alone and isolated as a flag atop Mount Everest, but we are not. Whenever we pray, our angels pray with us, adding their assent to our words of worship or praise or blessing, and adding their own thoughts to ours when we give thanks or ask for help and rejoicing whenever we turn from the darkness to the light. We are never closer to our angels than when we pray to God. And in the quiet time that follows a period of prayer, our hearts are especially free of dark influences and especially open to the angels of love and light that God sends to us. We can hear what they say to our hearts more clearly than at any other time.

When we pray together, we have the added force of many angels joining with us. This can be an especially powerful way to focus on our need for healing. In Chapter Ten I describe how we can pray together with others and our angels to focus on healing. But remember this: whether you pray by yourself or with others, you are surrounded, as Saint Paul says, by a "great cloud of witnesses" who share their love and joy with you.

What more perfect climate could we ask for as we work to heal our lives?

## Chapter Six
# Healing Our Bodies

e are travelers in eternity, every one of us. We are immortal spirits, destined to live on forever within the providence of God. We are meant to grow and develop in all the areas that make us human (and being human is an exceptional glory) for ever and ever. The range of the universe is ours to travel; the depths of the mystery of God are ours to explore.

However, as long as we live on Planet Earth, we must still wear space suits: cocoons of flesh and blood that enable us to breathe the air, orient and nourish ourselves, and travel around. These space suits, unlike those of astronauts, are a very real part of us. They are tied in intimately to our minds, our souls, our lives. Nothing can affect one without having ramifications for the other.

An anxiety of spirit can become an all-too-real stomach-ache. A nagging pain in the back can become a worry in the mind.

We do most of our living on earth through these space suits, and yet, we all have experiences that reaffirm for us what we secretly know inside: that this world is not our ultimate destination. Sometimes we sense it in prayer; we know we are tied to God and to eternity by a heart-thread we cannot define or even verbalize. Sometimes we experience a moment of contemplation when the divine speaks to us directly, bypassing all words and concepts—and we realize we have always understood what the word-without-a-word is saying ineffably. Or it may be a moment when we leave our space suits behind to experience other realities we could never have known.

I think we can tell when we have such moments, because they're virtually impossible for us to describe. In *Touched by Angels*, I included a number of descriptions of angels that various people had seen. None of the descriptions matched, yet all were consonant with what little we know of angelic manifestations. What I sensed, what I know from my own experience, is that our senses are not discrete enough (or perhaps they are too discrete) to describe a being that is not of this dimension.

But what does all this have to do with physical healing and angels? I think we need to realize that our bodies are a very real part of our existence, a deliberate welding of flesh and soul for a time, for a beautiful purpose. We are not here as a punishment! We are students, and our angels are among our teachers.

Some of us have more effective space suits than others. For some, the space suit needs repairs more often. For all of us, however, our space suit will eventually break down beyond repair. This is called dying, and we fight it be-·cause for most people, especially for those who have not sought God or recognized the God-longing within, dying is something to be feared. Without those spiritual en-counters, we forget that this world is no more (or less) than a beautiful stopover, before we reach our final desti-nation. We think instead that this world is all there is, and we don't want to leave it, just as a baby fights not to leave the mother's womb.

This separation of body and spirit is watched over most carefully by our angels. Like midwives, they are present to help us through the shedding of our space suits and into the free limitlessness of eternity. They heal the shock of this most glorious of adventures, and lead us on toward the face of God.

But long before that event, our angels also function as the most skilled of space-suit technicians, helping us repair, or even repairing directly, flaws, both small and great, that may develop. I have already said that I believe angels most often do not wave magic wands over us to heal us. They prefer to teach us how to heal ourselves and to seek healing from others.

But sometimes angels do indeed intervene in a way that we would call miraculous. God sends them, as instru-ments of the divine, to touch our bodies with the healing light. I think the wonder of it is that angels never just bring healing to our bodies alone. Angelic healing reaches deeper than our space suits to heal the soul that dwells in partnership with them. Such is the story of Jana Riley:

\* \* \*

# Healing in Its Wings

## Jana Riley

*They say that angels are especially close to mothers-to-be, not only a woman's guardian angel, but her baby's guardian angel as well. Some believe that guardian angels take over when a child is born; I've long felt in the depths of my soul that a guardian angel is appointed the minute life begins to grow in the womb. And that guardian angel fights for the life of that unborn child as fiercely as that angel is permitted. Jana's story reminds us just how protective guardian angels can be.*

EVEN AS I COLLAPSED IN AGONY on the couch, my arms wrapped protectively around my abdomen, I was thinking, *This can't be happening to me!* The pain shot through me like an electric current, singing in my nerves, and I was helpless to do anything except let it flow over me.

It all happened just before Christmas of 1978. I was living in Carmel, Indiana, near Indianapolis. It was a stressful time. I was seven months' pregnant with my first child, and my marriage was all but over.

I remember when my doctor confirmed that I was pregnant. It was one of those bittersweet moments. Like most women, I had dreamed of having children, but . . . My husband and I were having serious problems with our relationship. We were actually planning on divorcing. Oh, there wasn't anything tragic going on. In fact, my (now) ex-husband is still a good friend and a fine father to our little boy. Still, it was not what one would have called a "convenient" time to be pregnant. But then, babies are not made to be convenient.

I knew I was pregnant even before the doctor confirmed it. They say you can't know at two and a half weeks, but I did.

I was thirty at the time, older than average for a first pregnancy. So when I first began having annoying little pains in my abdomen about a week later, I didn't think them particularly important. I remember the first time I felt the pain. I was sitting at the foot of my bed, when this sharp stabbing sensation made me wince. *It's probably normal for a woman your age to have slightly different experiences*, I thought.

But the pains continued, and, even though I have a high tolerance for pain, like any sensible woman, I went to my gynecologist. He assured me that the pains were not important, and the ultrasound showed that everything was normal, so I tried to go about my usual routine. *After all, doctors are trained specialists*, I reflected. *What do you know about it?*

Although I was able to work and do most of the things I usually did, it was a hard pregnancy in some ways. I found I was constantly hungry, yet I would throw up every evening. It was taxing and annoying. Imagine going through the same routine every night: eating, feeling nauseous, and almost looking forward to throwing up so I would feel better. I kept having cravings for apples and fish—foods I'm not especially fond of today.

As I grew in my pregnancy, the pains grew as well. By my seventh month, they had long since become constant, twenty-four hours a day. And they weren't dull aches I could ignore. It felt as though, every minute, someone was stabbing my abdomen with a three-inch sharp knife and twisting it in the wound. When I had first become pregnant, the area of the pain was just a few inches in diameter; by the seventh month my whole abdomen felt as if it were being ripped by the constant pain.

I had no idea what was causing the awful pain. There was no indication that the baby was pressing on anything; that would have caused more of an aching or gnawing pain. It worried me that the doctor couldn't explain the pain either. I had no idea if it was an indication that something was wrong with me internally or simply "one of those things." But two years later I had a bad bout of peritonitis from pelvic inflammatory disease, so perhaps that condition was already manifesting itself and I didn't know about it at the time.

Still, despite the constant jabbing pain, I had no worries for my baby. From the beginning of my pregnancy I had experienced a sense of confidence and peace that my child would be just fine. I think that my angel—or perhaps my baby's angel—was touching me in this way so I wouldn't be anxious.

Things came to a head in December. I had no idea when I went to fix myself a little lunch on that day that something so terrible—and so wonderful—was about to happen. Just thinking about it today makes me cry with emotion, with gratitude and love at the way God heard my cry for help and answered it through the angels.

I went into the kitchen to make a sandwich. It was a modern kitchen in a modern ranch-style home. I was standing at the counter, thinking about getting some food out, when the pain hit. Never in my life have I ever experienced anything like it: a sudden, searing, devastating explosion of pain. It felt as though my abdomen were being ripped open, like an old Japanese samurai committing ritual suicide. I thought I was totally rupturing inside, tearing apart. I thought I was going to die. In that moment I feared for my baby's life, too.

The agony took my breath away. I thought for certain I would pass out. Hanging on to anything I could, I staggered into the den and fell, rather than sat down, on the brown couch, my head resting on the arm. To tell the truth, even though the couch was only a few feet from where I had been standing in the kitchen, I didn't think I'd make it.

For the first time in my whole pregnancy I worried about the baby inside me. What was happening? What was going to happen? I began to be terrified, even as my body continued to be torn apart by the pains.

And then—just as my head hit the couch—it happened. I've often wondered if my angel, or maybe my baby's angel, was just waiting for me to lie down. I felt a heavenly presence, an angelic presence in the room. It was as though it came through the ceiling of the den, although I didn't see it actually come through the ceiling. In fact, although I saw it clearly, I didn't really see it at all. I can't begin to describe what I experienced, because it wasn't from this world at all. Words just don't exist in English, or in any language we can know.

The presence I felt was much bigger than I was, or maybe it was a light, an essence, a being, a totality. All of those words are partly true, but none of them is really accurate. I saw, but not with my eyes. I heard, but not with my ears. It was all beyond my senses, so much so, in fact, that they were obsolete, almost a hindrance, except that angels can get by all sorts of obstacles to do their work, even the obstacles of our senses.

But it was real, much more real than I am, much more concrete than any of my senses. In comparison with that spiritual presence, I was the one who felt light, of little substance. It was the *angel* that was real. In fact, ever since that experience there are times when I feel my five senses are a veil, a hindrance in touching the spiritual realm. It was as if everything in my life was in black-and-white, and the angelic presence was in Technicolor, or as if my life was an old scratchy record from my youth and the angel was a state-of-the-art CD in quadraphonic stereo.

As I watched, this being, this presence came down, as soft as a feather, and settled over me and around me, beneath me and within me, filling me with its presence and its love and healing. At once, all of the pain that was racking my body simply dissolved into the being's energy and was transformed. Like a mist or a vapor the pain melted away. To this day I feel that the angel came, not just to stop my pain and to teach me about God's love, but to heal my unborn child of whatever was threatening its life.

Trying to describe how that happened is next to impossible. I feel that the angel just saturated me with love, not like any love I've ever known or that we really can know fully on earth. The love was indescribable, but I knew it was love, love of everything, unconditional, unquestioning, all-inclusive. It taught me that love is not only eternal but infinite. It made me realize that love is the purpose and end of everything. Love is its own answer.

And yet, at the same time it was the most personal, most intimate experience I have ever had. I don't know how love can be infinite and intimate at the same time, but it was. It was awesome. Never in my wildest dreams could I have imagined such a love. It was as if this angel had loved different people and animals, and because it had loved them, had become one with them. I could feel the love it had had for each of them, and in doing so, they all became one.

While this angel was so totally permeating my being with love and healing, I also could sense something about its own feelings. Angelic feelings are not like human emotions. I don't think it *had* feelings per se; I think it *was* feelings. The angel was so totally filled with love from the Love that is the Source of all things that it seemed to me that it actually "was" what it "did." Action, being, energy, doing—all these meant the same thing.

What happened while this angelic presence was filling me? I'm not sure. I didn't feel anything in particular, except for the release from pain and worry. As soon as the being settled over me, I knew everything was fine, was perfect, was whole, was normal. I had an indescribable sense of total confidence that there was nothing to fear.

But when the angel began to separate its presence from me, lifting up, so to speak, from me, I felt the separation keenly. I wanted to go with it; the longing was sharp and urgent. In that moment I didn't care about anything on Earth any longer.

The angel didn't speak, yet it communicated to me

that I couldn't go with it. It didn't need to say why; I understood. But the separation was unendurable, and I said, "Please don't go! Please don't go!"

And in a gesture of love and understanding so moving that I still cry when I think of it, the angel came back once more and settled all around me, filling me again with the indescribable joy and light—just for a few seconds, and then it lifted up again, and was gone. It was so brief, and yet the memory of it is burned into my soul, an angel's healing kiss.

I don't remember how long I lay there, just bathed in utter peace and healing. I was so filled with love that it was some little time later that I realized that the pains in my abdomen were gone, totally gone. Even the memory of all the hurting and pain, all the fear and anxiety was healed. I knew without question that I was whole, that my baby was perfectly all right. The sense of confidence, of trust, was overwhelming.

And even more, I knew that the pain would never return. I had had it with me continually, night and day, for seven months; but I knew it was gone forever. And it was. I never experienced an instant of pain or even discomfort after that.

I finally got up from the couch, but so overwhelmed was I by that sense of being loved unconditionally by God that I have no recollection of anything else I did that day. I floated in an ocean of love, a sea of protection. I was carried along by a river current so strong and deep that I just wanted to go with it forever. It took several days before my ordinary senses and my awareness of what was going on around me really came back—I won't say to reality, because what I experienced is the true Reality—but at least to the world around me.

My pregnancy continued to term without incident. And, although the birth had some difficulties of its own, my son Ryan was born beautiful and healthy.

When I think back to that time, I realize that the angel who came to me healed so much more than my pain. So many things that people fear—aging, illness, accidents, death—none of these has any power to affect me. I have no fears at all. Even death to me seems like nothing more than a beautiful birth into an existence so full of love we can scarcely contemplate it, let alone understand it.

I never spoke with anyone about what I experienced that day. It was so personal, and, besides, I just didn't have the words. But I did share it with Ryan when he was of an age to understand, because I wanted him to know the part the angel played in his life. And he asked me an interesting question: "Mom, do you think it was your guardian angel or mine?"

I was surprised, because I hadn't really considered it. But the more I think about it, the more I feel it was Ryan's guardian angel, who came to protect him and heal him in my womb. That angel has continued to protect him and save him from harm ever since he was born.

And I've learned so many wonderful lessons, things I'll never be grateful enough for. I've learned that God is unconditional love, not some angry judge just waiting for us to slip up. I've learned that all things are filled with that unconditional love. I've come to understand that we are eternal, and that wherever we are, whatever we are, we are with God and God is with us and in us.

And, as beautiful and wonderful as my life now is, I long for the day when I will know the loving embrace of that angel once more, and never leave it again.

## Chapter Seven

# Healing Our Spirits

oul-sickness is not something we talk about much. We use fancy terms derived from medicine and psychology instead. But sometimes what needs healing is our basic orientation and attitude toward life itself, a flawed vision in our soul. It can manifest itself in addictions of all kinds, or in behavior that takes no note of moral or behavioral norms. It's as complex as each soul, each spirit, and it winds up affecting everything in a person's life: health, rationality, relationships.

This kind of basic misperception of our purpose on Earth results in great harm to ourselves and others. We may grow up with no self-esteem, so that we treat the world with scorn or anger. We may, on the contrary, think we are absolutely perfect, and that only our own desires matter, so we use people and things to get our own way.

Whatever the scenario, soul-sickness prevents us from living as we were meant to live. We destroy our bodies and minds with deliberate addictions, whether to drugs or sex or power. We build no relationships, make no ties or bonds with others, unless they are built on domination or slavery. Everything is wrong, because we are so totally out of balance we don't even know how to set it right. Most people who have been in the depths of addiction or alienation say afterward that a part of them was crying out for help, but they didn't even recognize it for what it was.

Thank God that our angels always do. They can touch us directly and heal us. They can stir up the pain even more, so that we must seeking healing or die. They can bring others into our lives who can help. Or, as in John-Ray Johnson's story, "The Grave Angel," they can do all three.

\* \* \*

# The Grave Angel

## JOHN-RAY JOHNSON

*I've spent most of this book pointing out that our angels generally work with us for our healing in quiet, unobtrusive ways, behind the scenes. This angel story is so far removed from the typical that it reads like fiction. In this case, an angel not only healed, but intervened so dramatically that I'm not surprised John-Ray's mother thought he was having the DTs.*

*Originally, I had planned to use it in* Touched by Angels, *but at the last minute John-Ray asked me to hold it back, and the angels sent me the inspiring story of Chantal Lakey in its place. John-Ray asked that I use a pseudonym. "I guess I still have a way to go yet in healing my memories," he said.*

I GOT KICKED OUT OF HIGH SCHOOL for good when I was almost eighteen for gambling. The fact is I had my own private casino in my school locker—portable roulette wheel, cards, dice, and all. I used to get a group together and we'd go out behind the school, cutting classes, and shoot craps or roll the wheel or even play a hand or two of poker. I was crazy about gambling, and I was pretty good at it. When I wasn't so good I'd cheat. Either way I made money. I suppose it would seem really penny ante today, but in 1966, $100 in a week's time for doing very little seemed pretty attractive.

Of course I didn't get much out of school, when I showed up. The reason for that was that I also liked to drink, and I was well on my way to becoming an alcoholic. I couldn't buy booze legally, but that was never a problem—there was a bunch of older guys who liked to gamble with me, and either they bought it for me or they used it to gamble with if they were short. I had a real good stash of hard liquor that I kept in the garage at home. I favored rum, the strong kind, and I would mix it half and half in a can of pop so no one would be the wiser, or so I thought. The can went everywhere with me; it even got to be a joke around the school, and kids called me the Can Man.

Anyway, one day in November of 1966 I showed up

for school late and drunk and was immediately sent to the principal's office. It wasn't the first time. In fact, I had been suspended twice since the school year had started, once for passing my can of soda around during gym, and another time when my English teacher saw some of my gambling equipment that I had foolishly kept in an open duffel bag.

When I walked into the principal's office, I found my English teacher waiting. I had hated him for nearly two years; he picked on me every time I was in class, or so I felt.

"You're in deep sh-t," he announced with a certain glee. "We know all about your roulette-wheel scams. The principal's calling the police right now. You're going to jail or reform school or wherever, but you're never going to come back here again."

"Sure, sure, man," I said. I had heard it all before, and I knew it was just a bluff. I guessed I'd be suspended for another week, but I didn't care.

Just then the principal came in, and I could tell he was angry. In a very few words he told me to get my stuff and get out, that I was not being suspended but expelled. "I called your mother; there will be a meeting about this, but you're through here. We've had enough. . . ." He went on and on.

In the middle of what he was saying I just turned around and stumbled out. I didn't even bother with my locker; I just went home and lay down on the couch. I woke up about three in the afternoon, sober and angry. Mostly I remembered the sneer on my teacher's face as he gave me the bad news in advance. "I'm going to have it out with that b———," I muttered to myself.

I took Mother's car, not that I had a license, and drove over to the school to see if I could intercept my nemesis. I was in "luck"; as I pulled into the parking lot I saw him come down the school steps.

Suddenly, something inside me snapped. I stomped on the gas and raced for where he was, meaning to run him over—and I did. With the right front side of the car I came up behind him and knocked him a dozen feet into the parked cars on the other side of the lot. Then I sped off home, where, fear and triumph mingling, I got good and drunk.

It wasn't long before the police came—I hadn't tried to conceal what I did. Before I knew what was happening I found myself in handcuffs and on my way to jail. I had never been there before, and it was frightening. I don't want to go into details.

The teacher was not badly hurt, for which I still thank God, but the charge against me was still attempted murder. And although that was later reduced, I knew that my life was over. I was facing prison, not just a youth facility. Even my lawyer didn't think I would get probation. I couldn't even get out on bail—the judge set it high because everyone was afraid I would go after the teacher again. Maybe I would have, I don't know. Anyway, bail was too high for Momma to afford, so I stayed in the jail reading and watching TV with the other inmates. It was boring, but after I managed to make some new dice out of bar soap, life became more enjoyable. I had more IOUs by the time my case came to trial than anyone in the jail's recent memory.

The day I was supposed to go to court, my lawyer spoke to me. He had arranged with the authorities that if I pleaded guilty to a reduced charge, he could possibly get me out of jail—provided I volunteered for the army. Well, that was a real surprise. I didn't like the idea of the army, but I liked the thought of the state prison even less, so I agreed, and that's what happened.

The next three years were a nightmare. Even now they're tough to think about. I tried to straighten myself out in the army, and I cut way back on my drinking for a while. Everyone seemed to gamble, however, so I started up my crap games and all-night poker tournaments. I had always had some skill as a cook, so in its infinite wisdom the army assigned me to the motor pool, where I was no use at all.

And then, the minute basic was over, my unit was sent to Vietnam, and I learned what hell on earth was all about.

I was in 'Nam for eighteen months, and what I saw there convinces me to this day that there is a devil and a hell. I saw it—every day I was there. For years after I returned I would wake up screaming, even after God's angel helped me turn my life around. There came a time when I did not know when the nightmares at night were over and the nightmare of daily reality began. I was on the front lines for about fourteen of the eighteen months I was in 'Nam, and I saw all there was to see, all the sickness and hideous wounds and bodies and death. I tell people sometimes that I think I lost my soul in Vietnam, and it stayed lost until God's angel found it ripped apart on the battlefield and reunited it with what was left of me.

To this day I don't know how come I wasn't killed or badly wounded during all that time. Because after the first few months, I stayed as drunk as I could, as often as I could. And I took drugs. I had never really gotten into drugs when I was stateside, at least nothing major. They just weren't readily available in our small town back then. But here it was different. My whole being cried out for escape, so I took whatever anyone gave me—grass, hash, cocaine, heroin—or what I could gamble for. There were a couple of times my company was in battle where I just lay down on the ground and went to sleep, with shells hitting all around me, I was so stoned. By the time my enlistment was up, I was as addicted to drugs as any junkie on the streets of the cities at home.

When my enlistment was up (I still don't understand how I managed to avoid being kicked out of the army), I returned home, where I sponged off Momma, gambled when I was sober enough to hold the cards without shaking, and slept most of the rest of the time. I was in the local jail on a more or less regular basis for public intoxication and other small charges, and I did some time for drunk driving. Momma tried everything to help me get sober, but I just didn't want to listen to anyone. I know I once said some things to her pastor that were so awful she changed churches for a while.

I was in such pain inside that I didn't care about anything in life. I felt so empty. I had no purpose, no energy, no mind. It was as if I had no soul. I saw myself as a worthless piece of junk, like a car in a demolition derby, not fit for anything except to be rammed again and again until it wouldn't run anymore.

I know this long tale of all my troubles may seem boring, but it's necessary for anyone to understand what happened to me when my angel touched my life.

In 1975 a cousin of my mother's died. She lived in a

distant city, and Mother felt that she should attend the funeral. For want of anything better to do, I went with her. I figured I could always watch TV in the motel or maybe find a new bar.

I'm not sure how Momma persuaded me to go to the funeral with her. Perhaps even then my angel was working on me. I didn't come into the church much; I just stood around in the vestibule or sat outside on the steps. But I remember that the hymn singing sounded so peaceful I felt guilty. Most of the time I tried desperately to avoid the burden of guilt and anger inside that made me want to drink and drug all the time.

When Momma came out we got into the procession for the cemetery. It was a hot, sunny day, very humid—it had rained earlier in the day—and the ground was soft and damp. I could see that a canopy had been erected beside an open grave.

Suddenly, I knew that I could not go any closer. I was so afraid I wanted to panic. Any other time I would have reached for my bottle or snorted a line of cocaine, but in deference to Momma's pleas, I had left them all back home. I realized that I might be having sudden withdrawal symptoms.

"Momma, I gotta go!" I said, looking around to see if there were any stores in the vicinity where I might buy some cheap whiskey. "I'll be back soon, but I gotta go." I saw the hurt and fear in her own eyes as I loped off.

I soon realized I was in deep trouble. My body was on fire with pain. It was withdrawal. I was terrified, but I didn't know what to do. As soon as I was out of sight of the funeral party, I fell to my knees, steadying myself on a tombstone, and threw up. I was as sick as a dog.

When I had stopped retching, I sat up a bit, leaning

on the granite monument. My suit was covered with mud and dirt, but I didn't care. Turning around, I looked at the gravestone and got a real shock. My name was on it! Well, not my name, but the same name, anyway. I later found out it was a cousin from my father's side, whom I had never known.

It was a terrible moment for me. It was like an omen, as though God were saying that I was doomed to die. I was so depressed and sick that I didn't care. But I heaved myself up to my feet, shaking badly. I believe I thought I would try to get back to the car and lie down.

It was then that I saw the angel who touched me and saved my life and my soul from hell.

I had been looking down at the ground, which was rough and uneven, not neatly manicured the way some cemeteries are. I didn't want to stumble. All of a sudden, I felt as though I ought to look up. When I did, I saw an angel standing about ten paces away, on a piece of ground that was slightly higher than mine. He was looking directly at me.

The angel as I saw him was very tall, maybe eight feet. He towered over me, even without the rise in the terrain. He was very bright, but I didn't see any light around him. Instead he glowed from within. I call the angel "he" because it seemed that way to me, but I don't know that the angel was masculine. He had short and curly brown hair and dark eyes that seemed to pierce me through, even at a stone's toss away. I felt like a rump roast spitted on a gas grill. I didn't see any wings, but the dazzling white gown he wore was so full and billowy that I could understand why people have always pictured angels with wings.

I was absolutely struck dumb at this apparition, and I remember blinking and turning away briefly as if to clear my head. But when I turned back, the angel was still there, looking at me.

My instinct was to run, I have to admit. I had seen some harrowing things in 'Nam, and I had run away from it all, through dope and drink if not in actuality. But this I couldn't run away from. It was as if my legs were rooted to the ground.

How long I just stood there looking at this vision I don't know. Finally, however, I seemed to come to myself a bit. It was as though my mind woke up. I've often wondered if the angel didn't sober me up suddenly just so I could take in his message with a full deck.

Suddenly the angel turned away from me and began walking away. Without thinking, I tried to follow and found that my feet worked normally once more. I stumbled after him, fascinated and fearful. I know I wasn't really thinking about it or what this apparition meant. I just had to follow.

The angel began to walk faster, and because he was so tall, with large strides, I had to run to catch up, until I was panting from the effort. He led me to a far corner of the cemetery away from the monuments and the funeral service that my mother was attending. And then he turned around.

In all my life I have never seen such anger on the face of anyone. It was as if the entire angel was one gigantic rage. The eyes were like two black pools, and the mouth was set in stern lines of anger. I didn't feel hate or antagonism or anything violent directed toward me personally, but the anger was unmistakable.

*What do you want?* I remember thinking in the instant before everything in me turned to jelly. But the angel did not reply. He just stood there looking at me, waves of anger rippling off him and washing over me.

*What do you want?* I asked again, wishing I could run away from this apparition.

Without saying a word the angel pointed solemnly down at the ground and looked briefly where his hand was pointing. I looked down, too, and what I saw made my knees give way, and I fell to the ground in utter shock.

I had almost fallen into an open grave. Apparently the cemetery staff were preparing for another funeral. I had not seen it because the sun was in my eyes. And although the angel said nothing to me, I knew what he meant: if I did not turn my life around, I would die.

I began to cry in fear, and I sobbed as I had never sobbed before. It felt as though my body and mind were being torn apart with convulsions, and I couldn't stop. I just collapsed on my side, hugging my knees and rolling on the ground in the loose dirt.

After some time I felt a hand on my shoulder, and I opened my eyes in panic, thinking that the angel had bent down to touch me. But it was my mother, deep worry on her face.

"What's wrong, Jack?" she said. "Are you sick?"

How could I explain what had just happened? How could I tell my mother I had just come face-to-face with an eight-foot-tall angel who looked like he wanted to punch my lights out for good? But I had to tell her, and between sobs and outbursts of tears I told her in a very hysterical way what had happened. I could see the lines of worry on her face deepen as shock and disbelief showed in her eyes. Later she told me she feared I was having the DTs or hallucinating from drugs.

I was in something like shock as my mother drove us home. I couldn't get the angel's eyes and anger out of my head. I knew, although I had never thought much about God, that the angel was telling me that God was very angry at the way I had wasted my life, and that this was the last chance I would ever have to turn things around. Just the whole idea was scary.

It was dark by the time we got home, and a part of me couldn't wait to get to my bedroom and light up a joint and get drunk. But when I reached for the bottle beside my bed, I just couldn't pour it out. I saw those angelic eyes and froze in terror. I lay on my bed in fear and finally went to sleep.

When I woke up, it was morning. I was still lying, all hot and sweaty, on my bed. I stripped off my clothes and stepped into the shower, feeling the cool water pouring off me. When I stepped out and put on fresh clothes, I realized how much better I felt. The images of the previous day were not as fearsome; I could see the angel's eyes in my mind without my stomach turning. I brushed my teeth, but the vodka in the bathroom glass tasted god-awful. I had forgotten it was there. I rinsed out my mouth with water, wondering what had happened. I had brushed my teeth with vodka for so long I had forgotten there was any other way!

And suddenly I found myself on my knees beside the bed, praying as I hadn't prayed since childhood. I told God that I didn't understand what had happened to me since yesterday, but that I wanted, for the first time in many years, to be clean and to live right. "I'm sorry for messing up my life. Help me, God, never to do drugs or drink again," I pleaded. And I felt better, as though one of the things the angel had meant by his appearance was to make me aware that I needed to repent of the evils in my life, not just stop doing them.

After a while I went downstairs. Momma had long since gone off to work, and I fixed myself something to eat. I wish I could tell you how weird a feeling it was, doing normal things like cooking eggs and washing dishes. I hadn't done any of those things in years. Even getting up at a reasonable hour and putting on clean clothes was a new experience. I spent the day downstairs doing some housecleaning and then weeding my mother's flower bed out front. I didn't want to go upstairs where all my booze and drugs were. I just didn't want to confront it.

When my mother got home, I had already fixed some dinner—nothing much, but I was out of practice. She looked at me strangely, as if she thought she could see a change but didn't want to believe it. That evening we spent together just talking about little things. It was one of the most pleasant experiences I had had in years.

Soon it was almost midnight. "I'm going to sleep down here," I told Momma. "I just don't want to go upstairs, I'm afraid."

With a hesitant catch in her voice, my mother said, "We could go up together and, well, we could get rid of *it*," she said.

I knew that was what I needed to do, and strangely, I didn't feel anything but the rightness of it. "Let's do it," I said, heading for the stairs. But when we got to my room, I still couldn't go in. "You do it, Momma," I said. And while I stayed outside and told her where all my stashes were, she calmly took all the bottles of booze and what drugs I had around and poured them down the john.

"I wouldn't have believed this yesterday morning," she said to me; and soon we were both crying.

Now that all the liquor and drugs were gone from my room, I entered it, and I could see how dirty and shabby a life I had led. I wanted to take everything in the room and throw it away or burn it. I wanted to make a fresh start in every way.

I told mother what I meant, and she smiled. "There's no time like the present," she told me, and she started taking down the curtains and stripping the bed. I began to empty drawers, and I filled a big plastic bag with empty bottles. It was nearly three in the morning when we finished, and during the process of stripping my room we found more drugs and more drink, which we disposed of down the drain. We had a final cup of coffee together; then I went to sleep. I saw the angel's eyes in my mind, and this time he did not seem quite so angry.

"Momma, am I really different?" I asked her a dozen times the next day. "Shouldn't I be going through all sorts of withdrawal by now?"

And of course I should have. Given the length of my dependency on both drugs and alcohol, going cold turkey could have even killed me. But instead I felt an increasing sense of freedom, as though the angel's message was not just "Stop or you will be dead," but "If you want to stop and be healed, God can help you, just ask."

For the first week after my life was so touched by the angel I stayed very close to home and far away from my old drinking buddies at the bar I used to favor. I called and told the guys I used to play poker with that I had been sick and wouldn't be around.

My energy level was incredible. In four days I cleaned the house, reorganized the closets, cleaned out all the gutters, repaired the shutters, and repainted all the trim, besides a hundred other small things. I was amazed at myself; it was as though I was finally coming alive. Even the awful memories of 'Nam that I drank to forget seemed to be starting to heal. I seemed to be undergoing a rebirth.

On Friday night, after dinner, I broached a subject I had been thinking about to my mother. "Momma, I think I want to go away to the VA hospital for some therapy. They have some programs for people getting off drugs. I need some help to get my life back together."

She smiled. "I never would have believed I'd ever hear you say that. I guess it really *must* have been an angel you saw. How else could you have changed so quickly?"

She drove me over to the hospital (my license had been suspended some time before) and I told them of my drug problem. It was surprisingly easy to arrange for some inpatient therapy. I needed help, not so much to break my addictions—the angel had somehow done that—but to help me learn to live again. I completed the program successfully and returned home. I never did talk about my experience with anyone at the hospital, though. It was just too personal, and, besides, I didn't think that anyone would believe that a drunken drug addict like myself could ever have seen a real angel.

That was nearly twenty years ago. While at the hospital, I learned something about the plumbing trade and found it suited me. In time I was able to earn my license, and today I am self-employed, happily married, and the father of a son. I have never taken a drink of alcohol nor an illegal drug in all those years and have never felt the need to do so, nor have I ever spent a nickel on a wager of any kind. I know that if I ever did, I would see those angry angel eyes that brought me the message I needed to save my life. I became a committed Christian, and I try to witness in a quiet way to the love of God in sending his angel to heal me, not only of my addictions, but of the wounds of spirit that had led to them in the first place.

Was my life touched by angels? It sure was, and not just touched, but changed totally. That angel healed me of a way of life that would have killed me for sure, healed my vision, and gave me a chance to start over again. When I was so far down that I didn't even know which way was up, God sent his angel with healing in his wings, as the Bible says.

I'm not planning to leave this world for heaven anytime in the near future, but I want to say that when I finally do, I hope to get the chance to thank my angel right in front of the throne of God. He deserves it, he really does.

# Chapter Eight
# Healing Our Relationships

e are surrounded, as St. Paul puts it, by a great "cloud of witnesses" to the use we make of our life on earth. Some of these witnesses are on earth; some are those no longer on earth, and some of them are those who have never been on earth—our angels. Each of us has at least one guardian angel, assigned to us when we are conceived, and perhaps others.

I have no revelatory authority behind this, but I also believe that our own guardian angels are our absolute heavenly helpers, that is to say that no other angels can just waltz in to offer their help without our guardian angels knowing about it. Rather, I believe that our guardian angels frequently call in angelic "specialists" to help round out their loving work in our lives. That is why I have always preferred to work as hard as I can on my relationship with just my guardian angel rather than with many angels. At times I can sense the presence and angelic activity of the "specialists" Enniss has called in, like Tallithia, who seems to watch over and enhance my creativity and communications through writing and speaking, and Kennisha, who is a special defender against the enemy (that is, the fallen angels, who are not at all happy that their lies and deceptions are becoming better known on Planet Earth). But I don't think angels are freelance operators. They are beings "on assignment."

I believe firmly that, just as angels are assigned to watch over and be guardians to each of us, so too there are angels who watch over and encourage relationships, angels who link us together with the bonds of caring and love. Our guardian angels, who coordinate all our spiritual guidance, call them in. These linking angels tie together and encourage many relationships, but nowhere are they more apparent than in marriage.

Many couples of my acquaintance, whether married or simply good friends, feel a linking bond, not just a relationship. They tell stories of how, when separated by many miles, they knew what was happening to the other, or they picked up the phone to call the other and found them already on the line. They call each other "soul mates." They are indeed "those whom God has joined together" and whom God keeps together, with the help of linking angels.

In Chapter Four I told the story of two friends of mine, whose love for each other took a terrible blow but who were healing through their own hard efforts and the help of the "angel of the marriage," as they called it. I had thought originally to include their story here, but since I became involved in it, I thought I would put it in the chapter on forgiveness to show the more usual process of angelic healing.

How do these linking angels work to help us heal our lives? I think they make use of whatever situations present themselves to try to bring people together who need to have a relationship healed, as they did in Michael Thayer's story, "The Angel Wore Overalls."

\* \* \*

# The Angel Wore Overalls

## MICHAEL THAYER

*Mike's story is unusual in that not only did the angel help him out of a nasty spot, but, just as importantly, it got him talking to his brother Clifford again after many years of virtual silence. Angels usually don't work so dramatically in our lives, whether healing them or saving them, but it's good to know that when it's part of the plan, they can and do. A shorter version of this story first appeared in the August 1993 issue of* AngelWatch, *where I was focusing more on the rescue part of the story than on the subsequent healing of a relationship.*

ANTIQUE AND CLASSIC CARS have always been the great hobby of my life. Even now that I am retired, I still work on them, and my brother and I still go to the rallies and all. I've won a few prizes in my day. But the real prize I feel belongs to my guardian angel, because one day, while

I was working on one of my cars, he came and saved my life. And, just as important to me, he helped heal a relationship with my half-brother that had gone so sour that Clifford and I had hardly spoken in nearly a decade. We had had a falling-out over, of all things, a car. In retrospect, it seems silly, but at the time and for years thereafter, it put us at each other's throats.

What happened was this: My brother was just as much an antique car buff as I. In our youth we had restored cars together and sold them. I had taken the profits and plowed them back into more cars. Cliff saved up for college. I went into sales and Cliff went into the Christian ministry. But he never lost his fascination for cars. I remember he used to preach a sermon that likened all the parts of a car to a person's life. One part of it went that a clogged fuel line was like having evil in your life so God's grace couldn't get through to start your engine!

Anyway, in the summer of 1972 Cliff called me to tell me that someone he knew thought he could get his hands on the remains of a Duesenberg, and was I interested in investing in the possibility? Well, for me, a Duesenberg was like the Holy Grail of cardom. So few are still around, and the price of an authentically restored Duesy is astronomical.

I said yes, even though it would mean an investment of about ten thousand dollars just to start (even the pieces of a Duesenberg are pricey). Cliff assured me his source was impeccable, and, although he had no money of his own to put in, he encouraged me to go ahead.

I met the guy who said he had an old Duesy, and he took me to a barn where I saw the car and met two other like-minded restorers who also planned to put in money to buy her. We wrote checks to this guy. . . . And the upshot of it was that we never saw him or the car again— or our money. The guy was a con artist. The Duesy was real, but it didn't belong to him. The ten thousand was virtually all I had saved.

I called Cliff, angry, furious that he'd let me down. He admitted he hadn't checked out the guy, but "he seemed so earnest," according to Cliff. He said he was sorry, but sorry just didn't cut it for me. After all, I was out all the money I had saved. We had a major falling-out, and for years afterward we scarcely ever talked; we spoke only at family gatherings where we couldn't avoid each other. Just think of it: two brothers living blocks apart in the same smallish town, and we never talked.

By 1980, I had gotten on with my life, although the loss of my money (and, to be frank, the realization I'd been conned) still rankled. My true love at that time was a classic T-bird. She was a real beauty, an original. Her turquoise paint still looked as fresh as when it was first applied. Her chrome still gleamed. There wasn't even a nick or a scratch worth noticing.

Only problem was, she wouldn't run worth a darn.

I had bought her off a friend, who had gotten her from the friend of someone he met at an antique car meet in upstate New York. I was determined to make her work.

Like any fanatic, I would come home from my regular job—as a department manager for a national chain— change into my overalls, and head out to a special garage I had just had built so I could work on my cars. It was my pride and joy—almost like a real garage. I didn't have a hydraulic lift, of course, but I managed pretty well. I had my TV out there, a fridge, even a little bar. I just about lived in that garage.

Anyway, one evening I was working on Robin (I called her Robin because of her color). I thought I had figured out the problem, and I knew I would have to take apart the whole exhaust system, a messy kind of job, to find out. It meant working under the car.

Then I realized that I had loaned out the ramps I used to raise the car up so I could work under it. But I really didn't want to put off the job, now that I thought I had figured out what the problem was.

I got out a set of jacks and looked around me for something to prop under the wheels. The closest thing to hand was a couple of heavy plastic milk crates. I turned them over and slipped them under the rear wheels, so that the tires rested on the upturned bottoms of the crates, and everything was perfect. I got my light, my tools, and crawled under.

I had unscrewed the clamps that held the muffler and tailpipe and was in the process of removing them, when I noticed that the car seemed to be settling. And before I could scoot out from under, the left rear wheel broke through the box it was resting on, so it was held off the ground only by the rim of the milk crate. Then the right tire followed suit. I hadn't counted on the bottom of the milk crates being too light to bear the car's weight.

The car settled ominously on my chest and abdomen, not hard enough to break bones, but pressing enough to make it hard to breathe. I couldn't inhale properly—my abdomen was squeezed too tight. I was in deep trouble and I knew it. I felt as if I was in the clutches of a python just squeezing the life out of me. I thought my back was breaking.

I called and yelled for help, but no one came. My

garage was separated from the houses on either side, and a belt of trees separated it from the houses in back. No one could have heard me cry; besides, I was too out of breath to yell very loud after a while. I don't know how long I lay there being crushed slowly by my car.

Just then, I heard a voice say, "Hold on, I'm coming. Don't be afraid." I remember thanking God and then thinking that I had imagined the voice—I was really in pain then. But the words were repeated. I just assumed it was my next-door neighbor Bud, a retired gentleman who often came over to say hi and share a beer with me.

Then I saw two feet and the cuffs of a pair of overalls. The next thing I knew, I felt the pressure lift off my chest, and I was able to push my little dolly free and out from under the car. I could feel two hands grasping my feet, helping to pull me out.

For a while I couldn't do or say or even think of anything. I just lay there gasping for breath and waiting for the great pain in my chest to lessen. When I had recovered a bit, I opened my eyes to thank Bud for saving my life.

But no one was there.

Then I remembered that no one could have gotten in the garage unless I opened the door, which locked automatically. I looked around and saw the jacks leaning against the garage wall, where I had left them after propping up the tires on the milk crates.

Then I saw the car. It wasn't jacked up with anything! The tires still stuck through the broken crate bottoms. The clearance was only a few inches off the garage floor.

How had I gotten free? Who had lifted the car up so I could get out? And why hadn't he stayed around so I could thank him?

I lay there, confused and full of pain. Had I imagined it? Had I just rolled myself out? I took one look at the front of my overalls, torn and scratched, and coated with dirt and oil, and I knew I had been stuck under the car.

I tried to get myself up, but I couldn't. The pains in my chest were too severe. It had me worried. And there was a numbness in my legs, although I could move them a bit. I began to panic, wondering if the car could have broken my back, or worse.

My arms still worked, so I rolled on the dolly over to the phone. In one corner of the garage I had put an old sofa, and a phone was on the nearby table. I had all the numbers of parts dealers and fellow hobbyists pro-grammed in. It was all I could do to reach up and pull the phone down to me. I probably should have called the police right off, but I couldn't remember the number. I have a terrible memory for dates and phone numbers and things like that. I could remember only one num-ber, and I couldn't even remember whose number it was. I thought it was my sister's. I only remembered it because all the digits were the same.

I punched in the numbers, praying someone would answer. And someone did. It was Clifford, of all people. He had gone over to our sister's house just on a whim, as he put it; in fact, she wasn't even home. He had let himself in and was watching television when I called.

I was in too much pain and too frightened to care whose voice it was on the other end that said, "Hello?"

"Clifford—Mike—help—my car." I couldn't say much more than that.

Clifford tried to ask some questions on the other end, obviously concerned, but I couldn't answer any more. "Help—me," was all I could answer.

"I'm coming," he said, and then the line went dead.

I sighed with relief, feeling much more calm now that I had made contact with someone. I remember going over in my mind all that happened, wondering again and again who had lifted the car off my chest.

About fifteen minutes later I heard a car pull into my long driveway and the sound of a door, a heavy one, being opened and closed quickly. I knew Clifford has a station wagon, so I guessed it was him. But when he didn't come, I began to panic. It hadn't occurred to me to think he'd check the house first. Finally I heard footsteps running on the gravel and then a pounding at the garage door.

"Mike! Are you in there?"

I called out to him, and the next minute I heard the sound of breaking glass. He had had to break the small window in the door in order to turn the handle from inside.

Clifford dropped to his knees beside me while I gasped out what had happened—at least up till the part about how I got out from under. I saw him look anxiously at the T-bird, its undercarriage just a few inches off the ground. But he didn't say anything.

With his help I managed to roll off the dolly and onto my side. "Let me call for an ambulance," Cliff said.

"No, I think I'll be all right." And gradually the pain began to diminish. I got to my knees with Clifford's help (and no doubt God's, too—Clifford was praying aloud almost every minute), then I was able to stand, although I was still doubled over. With him supporting me every inch of the way, we made it to his car. The tires spat gravel as he headed for the county hospital twenty miles away.

We didn't talk much, but I was so grateful to Clifford for coming to get me that I forgot all about my long feud with him. He took charge quietly, and it was not until I was waiting to go into X-ray that I told him how I had been rescued.

"You're going to think I'm crazy, Cliff, but this man came out of nowhere, got into my locked garage, lifted the car right off me, and pulled me free. And then he vanished into thin air."

My brother smiled. "You're not crazy, Mickey," he said. "Because that was no man—it was your guardian angel. God sent him to help you."

I was surprised by Clifford's answer, even though, since he is a minister, I guess it was a likely one for him. I didn't have much time to think about it, though. At that moment the technicians wheeled me into X-ray.

The news was pretty good. I didn't have any broken bones or internal bleeding. The doctors figured I had bruised kidneys and some badly sprained areas around the rib cage (which were responsible for the pain—I thought I was having a heart attack, it was so bad). In the end, they kept me overnight.

Throughout it all, Clifford stayed right beside me. As I listened to him talk about his church, his work, people he had met, I found it harder and harder to maintain my longtime resentment at the misunderstanding that had lost me the money. Over the years I had built up an image in my mind of a brother who had deliberately deceived me, who was secretly competing with me, who deep down wanted me to lose my money, maybe even a brother who had conspired with the con man to get me involved. Now I realized that all I had thought about was

147

a bad fantasy, a nightmare. It wasn't real. Clifford was just Clifford, and I realized I loved him.

I guess it was being flat on my back in a hospital bed and having nowhere to go, nothing to do, nothing I could do except listen to my brother that helped heal my old resentment. I finally said, during a lull in Cliff's narrative, "Cliff, I'm sorry. . . ."

"It's okay," Cliff said, patting me on the shoulder. "We can talk about it tomorrow when you get out of here. We'll work it out."

Cliff was as good as his word. The next morning, even though it was a Sunday, he came to pick me up. He had called in a substitute minister to take his services. "You're coming to my house," he announced flatly.

"But what about the garage, the broken window? I've got to fix it," I started to argue.

"Albert [our sister's husband] fixed the window last night and everything is locked up."

I spent two days with Clifford, two very enlightening days. All my old assumptions fell away one by one, all my anger and resentment faded more and more. And Cliff said the same thing about himself. He had built up in his mind the image of a brother so prejudiced against him that he had never even tried very hard to overcome it. He told me a long time afterward that he had never realized how his own pastoral work had been hampered by having such an unhealed relationship in his life.

I wish I could describe the peace that surrounded my day in the hospital and the two days I spent with Clifford. In retrospect, I can believe that angels of healing were there, lending an atmosphere of love and forgiveness. We talked and talked, and every time one of us came close to being bitter or angry, we would see the light and we would laugh. All our resentments and anger just began to fall away. We didn't even need to go digging deeply into motivations and all; it just wasn't necessary. Although we didn't know how to use formal words like "Will you forgive me?" we did forgive each other. By the time Clifford drove me home, we had started to catch up on years of lost memories and events, and we had a few new ones to share.

We pulled into the driveway and went into the garage. Viewing my Robin, still stuck in her milk crates, I remembered Clifford telling me that it was an angel. At the time, it just struck me as funny. But you know, I really do believe him. It *was* my angel.

And yet, although I'm really grateful that the angel showed up to lift the car off me, I think the more important miracle was bringing Clifford and me together. Frankly, I think he orchestrated it all—not the accident, of course—but having Cliff go over to our sister's for no reason and then just hang around when she wasn't home. I think the time we had together and the peaceful atmosphere, and the way we just were able to get the garbage in our relationship out the door, was the angel's work, too. It's almost as though our guardian angels had been "plotting" how, when the accident happened, they would turn it to good, by bringing Cliff and me together.

My brother and I are better friends now than we ever were. And our reconciliation has had good fruits for our whole family—we all get together more for parties and birthdays, anniversaries, etc. Cliff doesn't have much spare time, being a minister, but when he does, we still work on my cars and go to antique car shows. I'm at peace, because that big hurting place in my life has been healed. And Cliff says the same thing.

But I sure hope that someday I'll be able to really thank that heavenly being in overalls who rescued me and brought Cliff and me back together.

## Chapter Nine
# Healing Our Planet

And to Raphael, God said, "Heal the earth, and proclaim the healing of the earth."

—1 Enoch

e live on the most beautiful world any of us know about—the Earth. From the Arctic to the Antarctic, from temperate climates to rain forests to deserts, this world is uniformly wonderful, an oasis of teeming life, both micro- and macroscopic, all of it foreseen with love by the One who is the Source of all love, all of it watched over by uncounted angels who have seen every cell form, grow, and divide.

Every region of the earth has its human partisans, too, who love and cherish it as do the angels. The native Australians who have wandered the outback for thousands of years, look at what to many others seems bleak and lifeless and give praise for the hidden water and creatures that sustain them. The Sicilians who farm the fertile slopes of Mount Etna seem foolish to those who fear a still active volcano, yet the ancestors of today's farmers called Etna "the breasts of the world" and loved her for the nutrient-rich soil that made their crops grow. If you asked them to move away, they would shake their heads uncomprehendingly and say, "This is our mother; how could we leave her?"

Death Valley, the Arctic Circle, the floodplains of Bangladesh, the peaks of the Himalayas—no matter where you look, you find the earth bursting with life. Scientists have found microscopic life-forms buried in the hearts of glaciers. The depths of the ocean, once regarded as lifeless because of the cold, the lack of light and oxygen, and the tremendous pressures, have now been shown to abound in complex life-forms.

All the life around us, including ourselves, has evolved to fit a niche perfectly. The balance of nature is one of the greatest phenomena in the universe. Just how is it that each plant and animal fills its role, giving life to each other in a complex chain of events that makes us wonder? There are flowers that look like insects, so as to attract real insects to "mate" with them and carry their pollen to other flowers. There are mushrooms that wait days for just the right breeze to propel their spores with the force of a cannon. There are mammals who control their reproduction flawlessly based on climate, temperature, and available food. One could go on forever and not come to the end of the wonders on Planet Earth.

But our planet is just as fragile as it is beautiful, and, due largely to human selfishness and lack of care, the earth is in deep need of healing, as are all the living creatures who dwell on it, ourselves included.

We need healing for our world, for the earth on which we stand and from whose resources we draw our life. Our bodies come from the earth, and when our spirit is freed from its space suit, our bodies return to the earth. In that brief interval, we draw our breath, we eat our food and drink our water, and we walk securely because of the earth and its resources. We are uniquely formed to live on this planet. So far we know of no other world that could support our physical beings without immense effort and the use of protective suits. To survive even on Mars, where the temperature at noon at the equator in midsummer is little different from that of northern Maine, we would still have to bring along our own oxygen and food.

But given what the human race has been doing to the earth over the past century and more, it may not be long before our world is no more hospitable to us than Mars or Venus. I don't have to detail for you what the cumulative effects of pollution, toxic waste, conspicuous consumption, destruction of environments, etc., mean for the future of our race and the precious planet we live on.

I firmly believe that one of the reasons for the incredible increase in angelic visitations is to raise our level of consciousness about environmental issues. The angels, after all, are the guardians of this planet, the gardeners, the landscape architects for God, as it were. There are angels who watch out for the plants and animals of this world, just as surely as there are angels who work with each of us human beings. Mountains, rivers, lakes, volcanoes, clouds, rain—everything that exists or happens on earth is watched over or guided by angelic activity.

For thousands of years, many religious and philosophic traditions have believed that God works through the angels to prosper our planet. Medieval Judaism believed this so strongly that they created thousands of angelic names to reflect the angels who cared for the planet. Thus we find Baradiel, the angel of hail, because in Hebrew בָּרָד, *barad*, is the word for hail. Among the Sufis, those who follow the mystical path within Islam, it is said that an angel descends to earth with every drop of rain to guide it to its proper place. The same mystics also say that it takes seven angels to create a single leaf on a tree.

I see no reason why this cannot be true. Naturally, I believe in gravity and all the scientific processes that cause the world to spin, to produce life, and to bring rain. But why cannot it also be true that angels watch over these physical and chemical processes, just as a researcher watches over the reaction in her crucible, even though she knows what that reaction must be?

I frequently go to a small lake near my home in the Watchung Reservation, a beautiful area of mature northeastern deciduous forest covering many acres of tiny hills and miniature valleys. But the lake is being choked by weeds, thanks to the silting caused by a highway construction project of a few years ago. By midsummer, the lake is only inches deep. I appreciate having all the wild sagittaria I could ever bake, boil, or make into salad, but that's not the issue. The lake is dying.

To make matters worse, the entire forested area is currently threatened with slow destruction because overpopulation of deer has destroyed a whole generation of new tree seedlings. The deer are overpopulated because the growth of towns and cities eliminated their natural predators. In fact, I'm writing this paragraph because I just saw a buck chasing a doe across my lawn—and my house is one block from a major New Jersey highway! Even the large Watchung Reservation can no longer contain the mating urges of the deer. As a result of overgrazing, the deer now munch on my lawn and on my daylilies. I had to fence in my flowers in order to ensure I'd have some daylily flowers for soup this winter. Many deer will starve to death, and a hunting season was even authorized in the reservation. The balance is all wrong.

One day I was meditating by the lake, praying about this local crisis, which is being repeated in many places across the country and the world. And I saw the angels of the lake and the trees just moving quietly through the woods, not in any sort of pattern, but each as they wished. It was a peaceful and exquisitely beautiful sight. I felt the love and devotion that the angels have for the reservation, and I was amazed that there were so many of them—thousands and thousands of angelic gardeners working, as they put it, "to give the plants and animals breathing space until humans can restore the balance."

But as I watched, the scene changed, and the angels began to walk purposefully together in all sorts of intricate patterns. And I noticed that their clothing was no longer free-flowing and multicolored. Instead it seemed heavy and it hung close about them. And, most astonishing, they all wore armor—helmets and breastplates—just like the old statues of Michael the Archangel.

I pondered this extraordinary transformation, asking for enlightenment from God, and after a while, I heard Enniss say, *These angels are the* guarderers *of this place.* As he spoke I saw the word in my mind, and I realized it combined both *gardener* and *guardian.* I asked him why the angels seemed so serious, almost sad, and he replied, *They don't like having to be soldiers, but the greed and uncaring of human beings has made them take up "arms" to help defend the planet.*

"Why don't they just heal the reservation outright?" I asked.

*It does not belong to us, but to you. We can and do work to preserve its spirit, but without your help, we can do little.*

It was at that moment that I saw what Enniss meant. We must work in partnership, we humans beings and our angels, if we want to heal the world and heal our lives. The angels cannot do it alone, because this is not their world. We cannot do it alone, because we lack the wisdom (and at the rate destruction of the environment is progressing, soon we will lack the know-how as well).

The angels of God love this world with a pure passion whose beauty could make us weep, if we were aware of them. They care passionately about this planet, for they have seen it form and grow out of the dust that once surrounded our Sun.

And when they see what we have done to the earth, they do weep—with sadness: *Stop,* they cry out, *Stop now! Stop throwing away your food, your air, your resources, your children, your lives! This is your world. You were set over it to tend it, and to tame it—not to rape it, to suck out its life and throw away the rind. Where will you go once you have used it all up? What will you eat when toxic waste contaminates your food? What will you breathe when carbon monoxide chokes your air? Where will you live when all the world is one huge garbage dump? Stop the madness that leads to your destruction, before it's too late!*

The angels are warning us that each of us has a responsibility and a duty to make the earth a better place to live. And they don't mean cosmetic efforts. (It's nice to pick up trash in the park, but the trash still has to go somewhere.) The angels want us to know that we must take a positive stand of whatever kind we feel most comfortable with on reversing our society's wasteful and harmful ways. We cannot be passive any longer. There is simply no time left. If we don't cooperate actively with the angels now to begin to heal our planet, it will be too late. We cannot leave this urgent mission to the next generation.

The earth is seriously out of balance, so is it any wonder that our own lives are also in need of healing? No, I don't mean to say that auto exhaust and landfills are the cause of everything evil. But the wanton destruction of our planet is part of a chain reaction that affects everything else.

Let me give you an example of a young married woman who, at the beginning of this century, worked in a factory. It was just a small plant, right in the middle of a growing city. They made watches. And every morning, she would take the watch faces and paint the numerals with luminescent paint so they would glow in the dark. She didn't know that the paint included the radioactive element radium. For more than a year she spent ten hours a day in this place, spilling the radioactive paint on her, breathing in the fumes, eating her lunch on the same bench where she painted the watch dials, twirling the paintbrush between her lips to get a fine point on it.

In the evening, the company would take everything from the laboratories where the radium was extracted, as well as dried-up leftover paint, and throw it out back in the field. It was easier and cheaper than calling in a truck to haul it away to the dump. And local residents who needed garden dirt were encouraged to come and get it from that field.

And they did, until for blocks around that radium-watch-dial factory, soil everywhere was contaminated with radium. People tracked it into their homes, they grew vegetables for the table in it, and their children played in it.

Soon, many of the women who worked in the watch-dial factory began to be ill. They lost weight and energy, they bruised easily, they were racked with pain.

They had leukemia, caused by constant contact with radioactive materials, and many of them died of it.

The factory closed, too late to help the women and their families. Nothing was done about the thousands of cubic yards of radium-laced soil until many years later, when they were finally scooped up and put into barrels by workers wearing the most sophisticated of protective gear. Many of the people who lived nearby were told that they had to move out, that their neighborhood was contaminated. It took years for a government, top-heavy with bureaucracy, to truck away the soil. It was so contaminated that no place would take it. No town would let them move it through their streets.

Finally the dirt was moved. The houses most contaminated were ordered destroyed. Most homeowners agreed because their homes had become unsaleable anyway. The lots where children had once played were fenced off—forever. And people were allowed to move back to areas the experts declared "safe."

And now, in this tiny part of the world, polluted by

human greed and uncaring, children are born with serious birth defects, and the rate of miscarriage is much higher than the average. Over three generations the rates for certain cancers are far higher than average, even among descendants of the original homeowners.

I should know. I'm one of them. All of this took place in my home state of New Jersey. The young woman who painted watch dials was my maternal grandmother, and the boy who played in the contaminated soil became my father, who lived near the factory and my mother's home. His father and two brothers died when he was still a boy. His surviving brother was sterile, and my parents were married eleven years before their only child—me—was born. My father and his brother both died of cancer. My mother and her sister both had it when they died. His sister survived cancer. So did I. In Chapter One I described my own bout with cancer.

And all of this has happened in one tiny corner, one little town in New Jersey, all because of the greed and selfishness and fear of those who washed their hands of the effects of pollution and contamination of the earth and left others to bear the results.

One small town, yet the ramifications are enormous. Thousands of people exposed to harmful radiation. The soil of a town contaminated beyond saving. Three generations of people adversely affected. A toxic waste dump halfway across the United States now stands guard over thousands of barrels of contaminated waste.

And this is not a unique occurrence. Television and newspapers are full of similar stories all around the country. I remember when I lived in Phoenix, driving past a vacant playground full of rusting swings, a ballfield with tumbleweed blowing across, a carousel turning idly in the wind. A ten-foot-high fence surrounded the field, and on the fence were signs that read KEEP OUT! CONTAMINATED AREA. DANGER! How long had the children played there?

Now think of Chernobyl. Multiply my family's experience by millions of times. The effects of the nuclear disaster in Chernobyl in the Ukraine have been felt almost around the world. Hundreds have died directly from it, and hundreds of thousands will have their lives shortened because of it. A thousand square miles of productive farmland are contaminated beyond recovery, and may remain so for centuries. Schoolchildren as far away as Sweden and Poland have felt its wrath. The milk and meat of animals who graze on contaminated soil is also contaminated, destroying the livelihood of thousands more. Geiger counters are currently the hottest item for sale in Moscow. An even larger area in Russia is contaminated by plutonium, strontium, and other products of experiments from the 1950s gone wrong. Almost overnight, more than fifty towns were wiped off the map. It's a disaster the Russians won't talk about.

But the worst threats have nothing to do with the horrors of nuclear waste. Just think of the ongoing destruction of the rain forests of the world, cleared without thought, to provide pasture for foreign cattle, for timber, for acreage. Why become upset at something going on thousands of miles away? Because we and the rain forests are bound together by an unseen link, and destroying the rain forests weakens the balance of nature. Destroying the rain forests destroys the habitat of uncounted thousands of species of animal and plant life.

Many people believe that the angels live in such a perfect society that their lives are filled totally with a kind of mindless bliss. I can tell you that this is not so. Of course angels live totally within the plan of God, and their own lives are not disturbed by our greed and callousness. But when it comes to their contemplation of the world, the angels, particularly those who work with the Earth itself and the creatures who live on it, are distressed.

Near my home in Mountainside, New Jersey, is the Somerset County Environmental Education Center, located in the Great Swamp. It's an enormous wildlife refuge in New Jersey, one of the last areas of its kind in the northeastern United States. Near it is the Raptor Trust, which rehabilitates birds of prey, many of which are endangered in my area. The center constantly offers programs to adults and children.

I have never seen or felt the presence of so many angels as I do there: angels of waters, of plants, of animals, of rocks, all speaking quietly with the visitors, and especially with the children. One night I saw them surrounding a pond where frogs were spawning, and they were dancing with delight. The peace was physical, the joy, unbelievable. Yet underneath it all, I sensed an urgency on the angels' part to communicate with a new generation the need to preserve our world and to reverse the destruction we have created.

The AngelWatch™ Foundation, Inc., the organization I founded in 1991 to chronicle the workings of angels in our world, is committed to doing all it can to preserve the planet. It uses recycled paper and vegetable-based ink to print its bimonthly magazine, the *AngelWatch™* journal, and it actively supports environmental protection issues.

I am, therefore, asking all angelwatchers everywhere

to commit themselves to the angels' cause: healing the earth. Rethink. Recycle. Reuse. If you don't need it, refuse.

Do whatever you feel called to do. But do it. Please. The angels are crying.

# Chapter Ten

# Angelic Healing Circles: Helping Each Other Heal

> Raphael said to Tobias, before he had approached his father, "I know that his eyes will be opened. Smear the gall from the fish on his eyes; the medicine will make the white films shrink and peel off from his eyes, and your father will regain his sight and see the light."
>
> —Tobit 11:7–8

e humans, as weak as we often are, have amazing healing strengths and powers within us, part of the largely untapped resources put inside our mortal frames by the loving God who brought us into being. How many times have you said or heard someone say, "I just didn't know my own strength" or "I didn't think I had it in me"? I think it happens to all of us at some point during our lives.

In every generation, some people not only have amazing natural abilities, but many other gifts that in centuries past would have branded them as lunatics or heretics. Psychic abilities, aura-sensing, second sight, etc.—all these have frightened people in their time, and people have called those who had such gifts possessed. But such unusual manifestations of insight and healing are in fact gifts from God as signs of God's love for all humanity, as long as we use them properly.

The fact is, we have scarcely begun to tap into the incredible abilities of the human species, talents and powers placed inside us by God. All of these gifts are designed to help us understand better who we are and where we come from, and to help us seek the God who gave them to us.

They also are gifts from each of us to all of us. After all, we are a human family, and we depend on each other to help us down the pathways of life. To paraphrase what John Donne said some 400 years ago: No one is an island, entire unto themselves. Each person is a piece of the continent, a part of the main.

Someone may have an intuitive gift to know where another is hurting emotionally. Someone else, just by holding their hands near another's arm, may be able to sense exactly where an injury is. Another may be able to see into a relationship and put their finger on the hurting place. I don't think that even the most enlightened of us knows all the healing potential of the human race.

St. Paul's description of the body of Christ in 1 Corinthians is a perfect paradigm of human society in general. He says in Chapter 12:14: "The body does not consist of one member but of many. . . . If the whole body were an eye, where would the hearing be? If the whole body were an ear, where would the sense of smell be? But as it is, God has arranged the members in the body, each one of them, as he chose. . . . If one member suffers, all suffer together; if one member is honored, all rejoice together with it."

This applies to us just as much in our quest to be whole as it does in our day-to-day lives. Although we have within us many of the resources we need to be healed, we also have an equal need to reach out to others and to let them share with us their own God-given gifts. Our angels can and do function as the go-betweens or match-makers when it comes to seeking help in healing.

We have within us remarkable abilities to help ourselves heal and to help each other heal. Every day we learn more about ways we can tap into our own sources for natural healing. Books on everything from laughter to biofeedback make it clear that our internal resources are a virtually untapped reservoir for healing. All of us, to some extent, have healing abilities within us.

It is also clear that different kinds of energies can overflow our own beings and be projected to heal others. Such gifts are called charisms by St. Paul, who describes this kind of healing as a gift of the Spirit in 1 Corinthians 12:9.

Healing, whether for our bodies, minds, spirits, or relationships, comes ultimately from God. In fact everything comes from God; God is the Source of all we are and have. God is the Whole from whom all wholeness flows, whether directly or through some other intermediary source, like another human being or an angel. If a doctor's treatment enables our body to heal, we thank the doctor, but we should bless God for the healing gift the doctor has.

Do you see what I'm getting at? Healing is a partnership that includes each of us, each of our angels, other people and their angels, and God, who binds us all together and who is the divine fire that lights all our candles, human and angelic. Certainly, God can and does heal people directly, and we have every right to ask God to work in that way. But it's been my experience that, most often, God heals us through each other, because we are a human family and we need to realize that we cannot live and die in isolation. And by "each other," I mean not only other human beings, but angels as well.

For this reason I have begun what I call angelic healing circles to help all of us, together with our angels, work within the providence of God to heal our lives. The circle is founded on the belief that God is a personal and loving God who wants all of us to be whole in body and spirit.

Because I am a Christian, the circles I lead all focus on healing through Jesus, who for me represents God in human form. Because my tradition is Catholic, I have no problem in addressing angels directly during prayer (clearly acknowledging the obvious difference between God and a created being). If you find any of the parts of the circle at variance with your own religious or philosophical background, you will need to be creative and change them.

# Forming an Angelic Healing Circle

## What is an angelic healing circle?

A healing circle is a liturgical ceremony, in which we, together with, as we believe, our angels, worship God and specifically seek God's healing light for our lives. By liturgical, I mean a gathering with formalized words, gestures, and ritual that those who are part of the liturgy perform together. The word *liturgy* comes from two Greek terms that mean "the work of the people."

## What is the purpose of a healing circle?

An angelic healing circle is designed to bring people together to pray to God for healing in our lives, and to ask our angels to help us be open and receptive to the healing that God wants for each of us. There's nothing magical about it. In fact, the model for it is analogous to small, home-based prayer meetings common to a number of religious traditions. I think the main difference is that in a healing circle we ask and expect our guardian angels and other angels of healing to be a concrete part of our gathering, and to participate by helping minister God's healing to each of us. But it is essential that all prayers, not only of worship and praise, but of petition for healing, be addressed to God, from whom healing comes.

## Should healing circles be held regularly?

A healing circle can be ongoing or a one-time thing. When I give workshops, we will sometimes end with a healing circle, and I find that generally people put a great deal of energy into it, even if they have never been in such a situation before. However, I do think that the most effective circles are ongoing ones, in which the participants know each other and feel comfortable with each other.

## How many people can be involved?

A healing circle should have at least four people, but no more than about ten. It's hard to constitute a circle with fewer than four people, and hard to give each one time to express their healing needs and to pray with them if there are more than ten or so. If more than twelve come to any healing circle, I generally have the group divide into two smaller circles once the opening prayers are completed, and then reassemble for the closing.

## Where should a healing circle be held?

Any place relatively free of distractions will do. That means that if you hold it out-of-doors, the weather should be pleasant and annoyances like mosquitoes and gnats and rumbling trucks should not be a problem. If you hold it indoors, participants should be free from having to go to the phone, answer the door, or tend young children, if possible.

## Is evening better than morning for a healing circle?

Any time of day can be suitable, if all the participants agree, but each lends a different quality to the circle. A healing circle held at dawn tends to be very contemplative, but with a lot of mental activity on the part of the participants. A circle during the morning or afternoon hours tends more toward the practical, the lively, even the humorous, but it's harder to keep focused. In the evening, people are quieter, more emotional, and less thoughtful. A healing circle held very late at night can be extremely powerful, but it needs an exceptionally strong leader who is skilled in discernment of spirits, because when people are tired, it is easier for spirits that do not want our healing to try to work their mischief.

## Who should attend a healing circle?

Healing is meant for everyone who needs to be healed, and that is all of us. But a healing circle may not be for everyone, because its dynamics can be rather intense. People need to come to the circle aware of something in their lives that needs healing; they need to be able to mention it aloud and to ask God for that healing; and they need to accept the prayers of others and the laying on of hands as a means to facilitate healing. In short, they need to be willing to open up and admit their need for healing.

Sometimes people come to a healing circle with expectations that their angels will just zap them with God's healing, whether for a bad relationship or a bad cold, and when it doesn't happen as they expected, they're disappointed. I remember one woman who had a chronic sinus problem. She had been to a number of doctors, who had assured her that she had no organic problem they could diagnose. She came with a friend to an angel workshop I once gave, at the end of which we held a healing circle. When the circle came around to her, she asked us to pray with the angels to God for healing of this sinus condition. We did, but one of the other people in the circle said, "I feel we need to pray for openness to forgiving, not just for a physical healing." She had been given what in Christian teaching is called a "word of knowledge," a special spiritual understanding of the underlying reason for something, in this case, for the woman's ailment.

We prayed accordingly, and, as I expected, saw no improvement in the woman's condition, because she said she couldn't understand what the message might mean—there was nothing in her life she needed to forgive. Nonetheless, the person who had spoken about forgiveness felt that healing had been given by God through the angels; she had a clear perception in her mind of the woman's angel coming to her and giving her a prism, which she felt was symbolic of increased understanding. But the woman herself felt uncomfortable, and when the circle was finished, she expressed some strong reservations to me about what had transpired. I asked her to be patient and reminded her that very few healings in life are instantaneous, because most healing involves understanding and wisdom.

I did not see her again, but about two months later the friend who had brought her attended a book signing I was doing, and she told me an interesting story. A couple of days after the healing circle, the woman was on her way to the supermarket when she suddenly began thinking about an older half-brother who used to abuse her physically when she was a child; once he even broke her nose. She tried not to think about him, but he kept coming to mind, together with her memories of all the abuse she had taken from him. She had never talked about it, and it had remained inside her, festering.

She was in the parking lot of the supermarket, her head throbbing from sinus pain, when she couldn't take it anymore. She sat there in her car crying, the memories pouring over her, and she thought about what the woman had said during the prayer circle about forgiveness.

Suddenly, she heard the voice of her angel saying, *You can let go now; you're safe. Don't be afraid.* And she realized that much of her pain over the years had to do—not with sinus infections—but with unresolved anger at the broken nose her brother had given her when she was a child, and the lie about falling down the stairs she had told her mother because she was afraid to tell the truth.

She sat there in the car for nearly an hour, she said, enlightenment and wisdom from God bathing her in healing as she understood what she needed healing for. And she asked God for that healing, and began the process of forgiveness. When she was finished, she realized her sinus headache was much less bothersome.

Ultimately, her complete healing took some time. After all, the wounds she had suffered in her spirit had taken a long time to be created. But in the end, healing her spirit led to the physical healing that was the symptom, rather than the cause.

### Who should lead a healing circle?

The Spirit of God is the real "leader" of every healing circle, if we enter into our prayer with the right spirit. But a human facilitator is important, too, someone who understands that God is in charge of healing circles, not humans or angels, someone who is not a control freak. A facilitator has to have a great deal of sensitivity to the people who make up the circle, as well as to the Spirit who guides it. Discernment is important, because it's often hard to see where the real needs for healing are. A facilitator above all must be humble, because he or she needs healing just as surely as everyone else in the circle.

## What is needed for the circle?

You will need to set chairs in a circle, close enough so people can hold hands, far enough so that each feels as though they have a little space. If at all possible, set up the circle of chairs in a location other than where people will socialize before or after the circle. The idea is to establish a sense of what is called sacred space. Try to use chairs that are all the same. If everyone feels absolutely comfortable sitting on the floor or ground, that's certainly all right, too. You can set up the chairs around a round table, such as a dining room table, or you can put a small table in the center of the circle. If you want to use a tablecloth and add flowers, that's fine. But please do not add any icons, e.g., statuettes of angels or cute cherubs or the like. The candles (next paragraph) are meant to be the focal point.

You will also need a large pillar candle on the table. It makes no difference what the color. My preference is lavender, because that's my favorite color. Some people prefer rainbow colors, to remind people that God, whose Light is represented by the candle, encompasses all colors. The candle should be lit by the facilitator before anyone else arrives. It will remain lit throughout the gathering. (If you are holding your circle out-of-doors, use a candle with a clear glass chimney so that the wind will not put out the light.)

You will also need a slightly smaller unlit pillar candle to represent the participants' focus on healing, as well as smaller white candles for each person. You might want to push each small candle through a circle of paper to prevent drips. The small candles can be placed on the table until people are ready to start the circle.

You will also need a third pillar candle, preferably one in the shape of an angel. If you cannot obtain one, use a candlestick or candle ring in the shape of an angel.

You will need a music source, preferably a tape deck or CD player. I have found that it's better to use recorded music than live music. I have been a professional and semiprofessional folksinger and guitarist in my day, so at first I tried playing background music on my guitar during the healing circles. However, I found I couldn't concentrate on two things at once, so I gave up on that and now use a tape deck. If you hold your circle outside, make sure the batteries are fresh!

As far as music itself, any suitable instrumental or very muted vocal will do. In the classical vein I like the French Impressionist composers like Debussy, Fauré, and Ravel. I am especially fond of Gregorian chant, because it is the type of music I sing whenever I begin to meditate. (However, since learning not only Latin but the breathing and meditative techniques that accompany the chant takes a long time to achieve, use a recording instead of trying to sing the chants yourselves. I would suggest any of the chants as sung by the monks and nuns themselves, rather than by a professional choir or a New Age interpretation, which are not at all authentic. You may need to experiment.) Many New Age instrumentals will work, too.

As far as lighting goes, if you are holding a healing circle indoors during the evening, try to keep the artificial lighting to a minimum—a discreet lamp in the corner, perhaps, but please avoid harsh overhead lighting.


## *Beginning the Circle*

I try not to begin a circle until everyone has arrived, particularly if the circle is just getting established. When everyone has come, the leader should ask people to take their places. At that point someone should begin the music. I like to choose a single piece of about five minutes' length. During the music people should begin to settle themselves and to breathe deeply and quietly, with their eyes closed. If this is the first time people are together for a healing circle, the leader should offer a few words about how to ground one's self.

Because we work together with our angels to focus the healing love of God, we need to be quiet and peaceful, so it's important to begin with meditation. It's not necessary to be in a deep meditative state; rather the purpose is to gather one's energies together. After all, when one addresses God in prayer, it is important to be as totally "present" as possible.

As the music ends, the leader should say a few words of welcome and about the purpose of the circle, for example:

> *We have come together to seek wholeness, the total health of mind, body, spirit, and relationships that is our destiny as the children of God. In this circle, we will ask*

*God to send the angels of healing to be with us, to enlighten us with God's grace so that we may know what kinds of healing we need and have the insight necessary to achieve them.*

The leader then continues:

*God is light, and those who walk in the light are filled with light. We ask you, loving God, to fill our hearts and minds with your healing light, so that all within us may be whole.*

At this point, someone should pass out to everyone the small candles on the table. Everyone should take their small candle and together, not one by one, should light it from the large candle that symbolizes the light of God, and then they return to their seats.

At this point I usually lead a short meditation in which the participants visualize the light from the large candle and from their own surrounding them all in a single bubble or canopy of protective light. I explain that this light is the presence of the Holy Spirit, and that everyone should do their best to renounce or give up anything they know inside themselves to be of the darkness and not of the light—hatred, greed, envy, violence, prejudice, egotism, malice, etc., so as to be more open to healing. During the time the meditation lasts, music can be played.

When the meditation is over, the leader says:

*Now we will light the candle that represents our desire for healing, our desire to be whole, our longing to be free to be all that God's loving plan has in store for us.*

Then everyone should, together, light the smaller pillar candle and return to their seats. People who wish to offer personal prayers aloud should do so, keeping in mind that our prayers for healing are addressed to God, rather than to the angels.

## Invocation of the Angels

In a healing circle we consciously call upon our own guardian angels to be present with us in a powerful way, to echo our prayers to God for healing, and to be God's instruments for our healing.

Within the Catholic and certain other traditions, the litany is a powerful way to focus the minds of a group on a particular intention. For the healing circle, I have adapted several litanies in honor of the angels, which are used for personal devotion. In a litany, a single voice makes the petitions or invocations, and everyone responds together. Sometimes you may want to have the leader read all the invocations; at other times you may want to go around the circle, with each person in turn reading one invocation and everyone responding.

## Litany of the Angels of Healing

God has given his angels
   charge over you

> *To guard you in all your*
> *ways.*

Upon their hands they
will bear you up,

*Lest you strike your foot*
*against a stone.*

O God, loving Creator of
all,

*Send your angels to be with*
*us, we pray.*

Lord Jesus Christ,
Redeemer of the
human race,

*Send your angels to be with*
*us, we pray.*

Most Holy Spirit, giver of
enlightenment and
peace,

*Send your angels to be with*
*us, we pray.*

That we might be healed
of all our physical
ailments,

*Send your angels to be with*
*us, we pray.*

That we might be healed
of all wounds of heart
and spirit,

*Send your angels to be with*
*us, we pray.*

That we might be healed
of all that separates us

from You, from each
other, and from our
own selves,

> *Send your angels to be with*
> *us, we pray.*

That we might forgive all
who have hurt us, as
we hope for their
forgiveness and yours,

> *Send your angels to be with*
> *us, we pray.*

That we might work to
heal the Earth,

> *Send your angels to be with*
> *us, we pray.*

Holy Angels, our
guardians on Earth,

> *Be with us and help us to*
> *be healed.*

Holy Angels, our
protectors in danger,

> *Be with us and help us to*
> *be healed.*

Holy Angels, our teachers
and guides,

> *Be with us and help us to*
> *be healed.*

Holy Angels, our
witnesses in heaven,

> *Be with us and help us to*
> *be healed.*

Holy Angels, our friends
and counselors,

*Be with us and help us to*
*be healed.*

Holy Angels, our helpers
throughout life,

*Be with us and help us to*
*be healed.*

Holy Angels, who love us
with the love of God,

*Be with us and help us to*
*be healed.*

Holy Angels, who bring
us messages from
above,

*Be with us and help us to*
*be healed.*

Holy Angels, who lead
our hearts to God,

*Be with us and help us to*
*be healed.*

Holy Angels, who want
us to be healed in
mind, body, and spirit,

*Be with us and help us to*
*be healed.*

Holy Angels, who
enlighten us with God's
grace to know where
we need healing,

*Be with us and help us to*
*be healed.*

Holy Michael the
  Archangel,

              *Be with us and help us to*
                      *be healed.*

Holy Prince of the
  heavenly host,

              *Be with us and help us to*
                      *be healed.*

Holy Michael, bringer
  of God's light and
  clarity,

              *Be with us and help us to*
                      *be healed.*

Holy Michael, mighty
  intercessor before God,

              *Be with us and help us to*
                      *be healed.*

Holy Michael, our
  defense against the
  enemy,

              *Be with us and help us to*
                      *be healed.*

Holy Gabriel the
  Archangel,

              *Be with us and help us to*
                      *be healed.*

Holy Gabriel, who
  enlightens our minds to
  the Word of God,

              *Be with us and help us to*
                      *be healed.*

Holy Gabriel, perfect
model of prayer,

*Be with us and help us to
be healed.*

Holy Gabriel, revealer of
mysteries,

*Be with us and help us to
be healed.*

Raphael the Archangel,

*Be with us and help us to
be healed.*

Holy Raphael, whose
name means "God has
healed,"

*Be with us and help us to
be healed.*

Holy Raphael, one of the
Seven spirits who stand
before the Most High,

*Be with us and help us to
be healed.*

Holy Raphael, who
ministers before God in
heaven,

*Be with us and help us to
be healed.*

Holy Raphael, noble and
mighty messenger of
God,

*Be with us and help us to
be healed.*

Holy Raphael, our guide
and protector on our
journey through life,

*Be with us and help us to
be healed.*

Holy Raphael, patron of
all who seek healing,

*Be with us and help us to
be healed.*

Holy Raphael, patron of
all who are healers,

*Be with us and help us to
be healed.*

Holy Raphael, comforter
of the sick,

*Be with us and help us to
be healed.*

Holy Raphael, who
guided Tobias safely on
his journey,

*Be with us and help us to
be healed.*

Holy Raphael, who
healed Tobias's father
of his blindness,

*Be with us and help us to
be healed.*

Holy Raphael, who drives
away the fallen angels
by the power of God,

*Be with us and help us to
be healed.*

Holy Raphael, who was
  charged to heal the
  Earth and proclaim the
  healing of the Earth,

*Be with us and help us to*
*be healed.*

Holy Raphael, guardian of
  the family and angel of
  happy marriages,

*Be with us and help us to*
*be healed.*

All you holy angels of
  healing,

*Be with us and help us to*
*be healed.*

Bless the Lord, all you
  Angels,

*You who are mighty in*
*strength, who fulfill his*
*commandments, and who*
*obey his words.*

Let us pray as Jesus taught:
*Our Father, who art in heaven, hallowed be your name. Your*
*kingdom come, your will be done on Earth as it is in heaven.*
*Give us this day our daily bread, and forgive us our trespasses*
*as we forgive those who trespass against us. And lead us not*
*into temptation, but deliver us from evil.*

*Amen*

Loving God, from whom we all draw life, human or angel, we come to you with confidence for healing, asking in faith that you fill our hearts, minds, and bodies with your light. Grant us the insight and enlightenment to ask for what we need, and the faith to know that you have already given it to us. In Jesus' name we pray.

*Amen*

At the end of the litany, the participants light the angel candle together, then blow out their small candles and return to their seats.

### Asking in Faith

At this point I often like to play an angelic vocal such as Eliza Gilkyson's "Calling All Angels"; Enya's "Angels"; or Amy Grant's "Angels Watching Over Me." All of these songs begin to turn people's attention toward their own healing needs. When the song is over, the circle is now open for requests for healing prayer. As they feel moved, people should speak up to voice their needs for healing. The leader can encourage those in the circle not to be afraid, whether they are asking for healing for a cold, a phobia, or an inability to forgive.

This part of the circle is designed so that participants can ask for healing for themselves. Requests for healing for others should be left for the second "round." After a person has voiced a need, the leader may say,

> *Let us ask God for this healing and ask our angels to bring that healing to* _____.

184

What happens next depends on the maturity of the circle. I believe strongly in the laying on of hands as a way of asking for and receiving God's healing. People who feel called to do this should make some physical contact with the person asking for healing, while all present ask in their own way, for whatever healing has been requested.

Because my own background is both Catholic and charismatic, I have been in many healing circles where participants have been moved by the Holy Spirit to speak aloud with unusual insights or wisdom that they have received from God about the person's need for healing. Sometimes people will have vivid visual impressions. Sometimes people will pray aloud or quietly in tongues— inspired prayers where the heart prays aloud but the words are unintelligible.

Any contributions that are loving, helpful, peaceful, full of clarity and light should be shared. Such things come from God. In my first book, *Touched by Angels*, there is a chapter called, "How Do We Know We Have Been Touched by Angels?" This chapter can be helpful in discerning the presence of God's holy angels.

After the prayer has been concluded, the leader will know when to open the circle to someone else. It is rare that a person experiences instantaneous healing. What generally happens is that God's angels mediate the divine light of healing through increased wisdom and enlightenment. The person being prayed for generally "feels" better, more confident, or less anxious about whatever needs healing, but it may take some time to understand what they need to do for healing to be completed.

Occasionally it happens that someone is so deeply

wounded that dark spirits can find an outlet to express hurtful or divisive ideas. If that happens, the leader should gently call upon everyone to unite in becoming more aware of the divine light that protects everyone in the circle. You can ask Raphael and Michael, who are especially powerful in binding evil spirits, to do just that. Sometimes, if all in the circle are comfortable with the procedure, you can pray for healing for the evil spirit itself, praying with love and compassion for such a sad being. In my experience, dark angels cannot stand human pity and compassion, and will withdraw, at which point the leader or other inspired person can offer a quiet prayer of thanksgiving to God, after which the circle will continue as before.

No one should rush the prayers for healing, and no one should feel forced to request healing. No one should ask any questions of the person making a prayer request. Sometimes healing needs involve others or are delicate matters that cannot be explained too clearly. It doesn't matter. God knows all things, and the individual's guardian angels, as well as Raphael, the angel of healing, know all they need to about the healing need.

Because people tend to put a great deal of personal energy into their prayers for others and in being open to the Holy Spirit for whatever wisdom the Spirit might want them to share, it often happens that participants are a bit tired by the time the personal requests are finished. A few moments of transitional conversation can help people come up for air, so to speak, before prayers for others' healings are requested.

The most helpful way is for people simply to voice their requests, and for one healing prayer to be made for all of them. Everyone may stand and join hands and ask

God to send the angels of healing and light into their loved ones' lives in whatever ways they feel moved to do.

## Healing the Earth

As I've tried to describe in Chapter Nine, our angels are actively interested in our efforts to save our planet from wanton destruction. This has led to a commitment on my part to join the angels' fight to heal the earth. I always try to make a prayer for the earth a special part of every healing circle.

While people are still standing, after having lifted up the healing needs of others, the leader will say:

> *And now let us lift up the earth, the precious planet we live on, to God through our angels, and ask God to show us what we can do to heal our world.*

Then the leader can begin invocations and responses asking for the healing of the earth:

Loving God, who created
   the earth in all its
   beauty,

*Help us to heal our planet.*

Send your holy angel
   Raphael to inspire us
   with both wisdom and
   practical knowledge.

*Help us to heal our planet.*

All you angels of God,
   guardian angels of
   people and animals, of
   plants and rocks, of
   waters and weathers,

                     *Help us to heal our planet.*

If anyone has anything practical they want to share at this point, any wisdom they have received about conservation and healing of the Earth, they should do so.

Just before the circle concludes, I like to ask people to sing together. My favorite song for this purpose is an old spiritual called "Peace Is Flowing Like a River." I have added the lyrics at the end of this chapter.

## *Thanksgiving*

People now take back their small candles. The leader lights his/her candle from the candle that symbolizes the light of God and passes the flame down to the next person, who passes it to the next, until all in the circle have lit their candles from each other. This represents our gratitude for the way God heals us through each other and through our angels.

The leader begins:

For the healing of our
   bodies,

                     *We thank you, loving God.*

For the healing of our
   thoughts,

                     *We thank you, loving God.*

188

For the healing of our
spirits,

> *We thank you, loving God.*

For the healing of our
relationships,

> *We thank you, loving God.*

For the divine light that
drives away the
darkness so healing can
take place,

> *We thank you, loving God.*

For the continued healing
we believe will take
place within and
without,

> *We thank you, loving God.*

For the compassionate
ministry of your angels,
who never cease to
work for our complete
healing,

> *We thank you, loving God.*

For the healing of our
planet,

> *We thank you, loving God.*

Together, all conclude:

> *Angel of God, my guardian dear,*
> *To whom God's love entrusts me here,*
> *Ever this day/night be at my side*
> *To lead and guard, to light and guide.*
> *Amen.*

At this point people extinguish their candles, and the circle of healing is complete. Since these circles tend to become regular events, there's always some socializing, often over refreshments, and usually an animated discussion about what people have been learning about healing and other subjects through the ministry of the angels. People may report on environmental projects they're involved in or share healings they experienced as a result of the previous healing circle.

I always like to leave the three candles—the Light, the Healing, and the Angel candles—burning in some visible place for the rest of the gathering. The host can put them out when everyone has left. Leaving the candles burning reminds participants that God's light still surrounds them, and that their angels are watching over them and moving them toward greater healing all the time.

### Peace Is Flowing Like a River

1. Peace is flowing like a river,
   Flowing out through you and me,
   Flowing out into the desert,
   Setting all the captives free.

2. Love is flowing like a river, etc.

3. Healing's flowing like a river, etc.

## Chapter Eleven

# AngelWatching™

---

---

ngels are at work all around us, a
prodigality of heavenly beings com-
missioned by a loving God to watch
over our spiritual growth and to over-
see the development of the natural
world. The Christian faith teaches
that each person has his or her own angel to look after
them, and to whisper in the ear of their heart about the
love of God.

The medieval Jewish rabbis taught that there was an
angel for everything—oak trees, hail, snow, silk, cheese.

Islam believes we have two guardian angels, effectively
doubling the number of heavenly helpers on Earth.

And all believe that, however many angels there are
whose work is on Earth, far more confine themselves to
the heavenly realms, carrying on the business of heaven

and ceaselessly worshiping God. The Moslems believe that the cherubim are so enthralled by the face of God that they do not even know that God has created the Earth.

Angels fascinate me endlessly. Someone once said that the proper study of mankind is man, but I'm even more taken with angels—who they are, what they do, how and why they do it, and what they have to share with us. Perhaps in heaven the angels, too, have a saying: The proper study of angels is humankind.

I believe that, just as we can see the beauty of God just by looking around us, so, too, we can see the activity of God's servants the angels by looking about. We just need to train ourselves to see and observe.

But how can we do this? I am often asked. Angels live in heaven, and that's far away.

I have to answer that I don't really believe that. Jesus once said to his disciples, "Look! The reign of God is all around you, in your very midst." To me this says that Earth, where we live and breathe and struggle, is itself a part of heaven, just as a vestibule or a porch or a hallway is part of the whole house, although it may not have quite the same character as the rest of the dwelling, and those in the vestibule can only catch glimpses of what goes on in the rest of the house.

And even more than that, as much as I believe in heaven, I don't believe it's in some other place. God does not reach down a hand through the clouds. The angels do not fly through the atmosphere down to earth. God and the angels are just as present to us as we are to each other.

The difficulty for us humans on earth is that our perceptions are so limited we find it hard to perceive the workings of God and the angels unless they are obvious about it. We are so burdened with our cares and troubles and with the effects of sin and evil that we cannot hear the voice of God or the quiet whisperings of God's angels.

Angels, for all that the earth is ours to love and protect and live on, nonetheless intervene regularly in our world and in our lives. We can know about them from what they do in our midst, whether it is protecting us from harm or inspiring us gently to love God and each other more. Like detectives, we can examine the angel's footprint, so to speak, and learn valuable lessons about who angels are and what their purposes are.

It's much harder to learn about what angels do within their own sphere. We have to rely on the visions of those who have been privileged to enter that realm and return to our own dimension, and those who have been inspired by the Spirit of God to write and speak about it.

I created The AngelWatch™ Foundation, Inc., three years ago to look for angels' footprints in the sands of time, to examine how it is that they work in our midst. Maybe, like Sherlock Holmes, I am the world's only "consulting detective" on the subject of angels. (Just joking—if you're reading this, then you're an angel-watcher, too.)

My purpose was to search, in every way possible, for the angels who are all around us and to disseminate that information, principally through *AngelWatch*™, the only magazine about angels in the world. (I checked this out, by the way. I did find a magazine called the *Guardian Engel*, and since *Engel* means "angel" in German, I thought I might have found another angel-interest magazine. But it turned out to be the fan-club magazine of Engelbert Humperdinck. However, on further research, I discovered that the name Engelbert means "bright angel" in old Germanic, so the research wasn't a failure.)

*AngelWatch*™ journal contains:

○ first-person accounts of angel visitations,
○ reviews of all new books and movies, etc., about angels,
○ serious articles about angels in many religions and phi-losophies,
○ informal articles on such subjects as angels in rock and roll music and plants named after angels
○ regular columns, including angels in the scriptures and portraits of angels known in history and literature,
○ editorial and letter-to-the-editor columns, and
○ a large resource column for further angelwatching.

The AngelWatch Foundation looks for angels in peo-ple's lives, in the religions of the world, in mythology and legend, in the movies and in music, in the newspa-pers and supermarkets. It actively seeks out first-person accounts in which people have encountered these heav-enly messengers, because the more accounts we have, the more we learn about these loving beings and the more we understand about God's plan.

The AngelWatch Foundation also works to bring peo-ple together who are interested in angels. A subsidiary organization, The AngelWatch Network™, serves as a clearinghouse for information and resources about angels all over the world. As head of this organization, I give talks and workshops about angels, in addition to writing and publishing the *AngelWatch* journal, which contains a large resource section to help people who want to network with other angel-related organizations and people.

As director of the AngelWatch Foundation, I have also found myself acting as an expert consultant, not only to reporters and researchers, but also to television and movie producers—even to greeting-card companies eager to find out whether people will want more cards with angels on them! And, more importantly, AngelWatch has responded to thousands of requests for information about angels and who they are.

The AngelWatch Foundation aims to research the nature and work of angels and to disseminate information on the subject of angels. It publishes a bimonthly magazine about angels, through its subsidiary, the Angel-Watch Network. It also provides an avenue for me to talk to groups about angels and to give seminars and workshops. I seek out and accept speaking engagements to publicize the work of the angels in our midst and to let people know about the foundation's activities.

Beginning in 1994, The AngelWatch Foundation will also make an annual presentation to an individual or to an organization whose conduct or activities is of such a nature as to make them truly "angels in disguise." The Earth Angel Awards will be given for the first time in August 1994, in connection with the National BE AN ANGEL DAY (see the Appendix under "National Organizations"). By honoring people who have acted in a way that is truly angelic, it is hoped that more people will be inspired to act in loving and caring ways and will be encouraged to perform good deeds for others and work to save the planet and make it a better place for us all.

The AngelWatch Foundation also produces and provides audiotapes, videotapes, and other similar material about angels, and maintains a library on the subject, which is available to researchers.

The AngelWatch Foundation has recently been approved as a 501c(3) nonprofit organization, something I have sought since the organization was founded. It is self-sustaining, through subscriptions to *AngelWatch* and tax-deductible donations. No one associated with it is paid a salary or receives any compensation in lieu of salary. About twelve dollars of each sixteen-dollar subscription goes directly to produce and mail the magazine every two months. The remaining dollars are used for purchasing resource materials for the library, paying for basic office supplies like paper and diskettes and toner cartridges, and telephone bills.

Needless to say, The AngelWatch Foundation is run on a shoestring budget. Should you be interested in contributing either financially or in other ways, your gift would, of course, be tax deductible as permitted by law. I would be glad to send you the AngelWatch "wish list," which describes some modest and some ambitious items the foundation needs.

If you would like further information about The Angel-Watch Foundation, or information about the *AngelWatch* journal, please send a self-addressed, stamped business envelope to: AngelWatch, P.O. Box 1397, Mountainside, NJ 07092.

If you would like to join the angelwatch and subscribe to the *AngelWatch* journal, the cost is $16 per year in the United States, $20 (U.S.) in Canada and Mexico, and $25 (U.S.) elsewhere via airmail. Checks should be made payable to AngelWatch and sent to: AngelWatch, P.O. Box 1397, Mountainside, NJ 07092. (Naturally, Warner Books is not responsible for providing these services and products.) If you know of someone engaged in angel-related activities, please invite them to contact me.

Remember, the more we learn from each other about the ways the angels are working with us and the messages they are teaching each of us, the more we will learn about God's loving plan for the cosmos, and the more we can be drawn into the mystery of divinity itself.

# Chapter Twelve
# Useful Reading: An Annotated Bibliography

his list represents a majority, but by no means all of the books on angels currently available in the English language. Because one of the purposes of AngelWatch is to chronicle the interest in angels today, this list includes a representative sampling of angel books from all beliefs and outlooks. The categories I have used are somewhat broad, and you may disagree at times with my choice, especially if you have already read several books on angels.

It's necessary to exercise one's critical thinking skills when reading about angels. Every author has his or her own views on the subject. Even books that are based on a particular theology or scriptures involve some interpretation of those beliefs and texts by the author.

Without discernment, we can read a book uncritically,

without examining whether we feel it contains truth or beliefs we are comfortable with. But if we read critically, we can learn about beliefs and ideas that may be totally different from our own and learn about a view of life we never considered before, even if we do not accept the premises the author accepts. Or, if you are only interested in books about angels that reflect a particular perspective, you can use this list to narrow your search.

Some of the books in this list do not appeal to me personally. Many espouse viewpoints very different from mine. But all of them were, I must believe, written by good, honest people searching for God, who, in the process of following their heart, discovered the angels.

When I give workshops on how to build angelic friendships, I tell people that they need to read a great deal about angels: who they are, what they do and don't do, what they say or don't say, because in that way they will be able to learn about their heavenly friends from the viewpoint of history. I hope you will be inspired to look for some of the books on this list.

Note: an asterisk (*) indicates that the book contains some material devoted to the subject of the angels and their role in healing.

# First-Person Accounts

*Where Angels Walk: True Stories of Heavenly Visitors*, Joan Wester Anderson, Ballantine. A classic. Highly recommended.

*Angel Letters*, Sophy Burnham, Ballantine. The first-person book that started the whole genre.

*Angels Among Us*, Don Fearheiley, Avon. A mixed bag of angel, ghost, and other stories.

*Angels Among Us, A Guideposts Book.* An excellent collection of stories mixed with attractive line art.

*Touched by Angels*, Eileen Elias Freeman, Warner Books. Who are angels, and what happens to people when angels come to touch their lives? How can you evaluate spiritual experiences in your own life and see if they were heaven sent? Also available in audiocassette and large-print editions.

*Meetings with Angels*, H. C. Moolenburgh, C. W. Daniel Co., Ltd. Scholarly book of encounters, translated from the Dutch.

*Angels of Mercy*, Rosemary Ellen Guiley. Lots of information in addition to encounters.

*Brush of an Angel's Wing*, Charles Shedd, Servans. A Christian-oriented book of encounter and reminiscences.

*In the Presence of Angels: Stories from New Research on Angels*, Robert C. Smith, A.R.E. Stories from the Edgar Cayce publishing company.

*Answers from the Angels*, Terry Lynn Taylor, H. J. Kramer. A solid book of experiences.

*A Rustle of Angels*, Marilynn and Bill Webber, Zondervan. A Christian-oriented book of angel encounters and information.

# General and Reference Works

*The Angels and Us*, Mortimer Adler, Collier Books. A philosophical enquiry into angels, written in a popular style.

*Angels and Men*, Ladislaus Boros, Seabury. A good introduction to angels.

*A Book of Angels*, * Sophy Burnham, Ballantine. This is the book that really started the flood of angel books. No angel library is complete without it. It is also available in a large-print edition.

*The Angel Book*, Ann Cameron. A good general resource on the subject.

*In Search of Angels*, David Connolly, Putnam. Good general introduction.

*A Dictionary of Angels*, Gustav Davidson, Free Press. An indispensable resource book. The bibliography alone comprises dozens of pages.

*Angels: The Role of Celestial Guardians & Beings of Light,* * Paola Giovetti, Samuel Weiser. This translation of an Italian work is an eclectic mix of metaphysical, Catholic, and artistic elements, with some fascinating plates.

*The Blessed Angels*, Manly P. Hall, Philosophical Research Society. A short but interesting monograph on the subject, with illustrations.

*The Many Faces of Angels*, Harvey Humann, De Vorss Publications. General book that includes such diverse sources as the Bible, Edgar Cayce, William Blake, etc.

*Angels: Ministers of Grace*, Geddes MacGregor, Paragon. Excellent, serious treatment from many perspectives, with bibliography and indices.

*Do You Have a Guardian Angel?* John Ronner, Mamre Press. Perennial favorite, written in a chatty style. A good basic book.

*Know Your Angels*, John Ronner, Mamre Press. Highly informative volume, easy-to-read style that offers interesting facts and lore about angels in history, art, literature, religion, etc. Good bibliography.

# Christian-Oriented Books

*St. Michael and the Angels*, Tan Books. A month of meditations and prayers dedicated to the angels. An unusual sourcebook for inspiration and reflection.

*The Angels: Our God-Given Companions*, the Blue Army (Washington, NJ 07882). An unusual pamphlet with the personal revelations of Magdalen of the Cross.

*The Angels and Their Mission: According to the Fathers of the Church*, Jean Daniélou, S. J., Newman Press. An excellent and highly readable book about angels as seen in the first centuries of the Christian Church.

*Angelic Healing*, Eileen Elias Freeman, Warner Books. How our angels help us heal our lives.

*The Angels' Little Instruction Book*, Eileen Elias Freeman, Warner Books. Enlightening words about angels, with accompanying scripture texts.

*Devotion to the Holy Angels*, ed. by W. Doyle Gilligan, Lumen Christi Press (Houston). A whole book of prayers and devotions, litanies, etc., to the angels.

*The Angels: Spiritual and Exegetical Notes*, Maria Pia Giudici, Alba House. An excellent book of competent scholarship about angels in the Bible and the Church, with good texts from unusual sources.

*My Angel Will Go Before You*,* Georges Huber, Four Courts Press. One of my personal favorites. He draws on biblical and Catholic sources and tells many fascinating anecdotes.

*Heavenly Army of Angels*, Bob and Penny Lord, Journeys of Faith. Very conservatively written Catholic work, focusing a great deal on apparitions of Mary and the angels, and the angels in the lives of the saints.

*All About the Angels*, Fr. Paul O'Sullivan, O. P., Tan Books. A good general introduction to angels in the Catholic tradition.

*Send Me Your Guardian Angel*,* Fr. Alessio Parente, O. F. M. Cap. A biography of Padre Pio, Catholic priest and stigmatic, who probably has no peer as an "angelworker." Fascinating reading.

*Beyond Space: A Book About the Angels*, Fr. Pascal P. Parente, Tan Books. An excellent, scripturally based book, with additional stories of angels in the lives of various saints.

*What Is an Angel?* Pie-Raymond Régamy, O. P., Hawthorn Books. A scholarly and philosophical book, but quite readable.

*The Angels*, Dom Anscar Vonier, O. S. B., Neumann Press. Very readable introduction to angels from one of the most spiritual Catholic writers of the century.

*What the Bible Says About Angels*, A. C. Gabelein, Baker Book House. A new edition of an old work. Hard to get through, and by today's standards, out of date, but still has useful material.

*Our Spiritual Companions: From Angels and Archangels to Cherubim and Seraphim*, Adam Bittelson, Floris Books. Interesting treatment, not really Bible-based.

*Angels on Assignment*, Roland Buck (ex Charles and Frances Hunter), Hunter Books. Evangelically based, with inspirational stories as well as Protestant angel theology.

*Angels*, Charles and Annette Capps, Harrison House. Ultraconservative, rather militant theology.

*It Is Written Herein*, J. Burton Dickison, Calvary Press. Reflections on all mentions of the word *angel* in the King James translation. It doesn't include all of the other mentions of angels where the word *angel* isn't actually used.

*Angels: God's Secret Agents*, Billy Graham, Pocket Books. One of the first popular books about angels, a rational, biblically based book of good scholarship and undoubted faith.

*Guardian Angels: How to Activate Their Ministry in Your Life,* * Roy H. Hicks, Harrison House. Biblically based, conservative theology, with some good angel stories as well.

*Angels*, Oscar McConkie, Deseret Book Co. Angels in the Mormon faith.

*A Handbook of Angels*, H. C. Moolenburgh, C. W. Daniel Co., Ltd. An excellent sourcebook about angels, readable, yet with good scholarship.

# Jewish Resources

*The Great Angel: A Study of Israel's Second God*, Margaret Barker, Westminster. A scholarly work with extensive bibilography and notes.

*A Gathering of Angels*, Rabbi Morris Margolies, Ballantine. Angels in the Jewish traditions.

# Metaphysical

*Living with Angels*, * Dorie D'Angelo, first Church of the Angels. Spiritual and personal reflections by the founder of the church.

*Ask Your Angels*, * Alma Daniel, Timothy Wyllie, Andrew Ramer, Ballantine. A book of speculations and meditations designed to help people touch their angels.

*The Angel Book, Angel Voices*, Karen Goldman, Simon & Schuster. A small book of aphorisms and aspirations, and a sequel, both with beautiful original art by Anthony D'Agostino.

*The Kingdom of the Gods* and *The Brotherhood of Angels and Men*, Geoffrey Hodson, Quest. Classic theosophical works about how angels and humans must work together.

*Commune with the Angels*, Jane M. Howard, A.R.E. A personal statement of her experiences with angels and ways of developing a personal relationship with angels.

*Working with Angels*, * Robert Leichtman and Carl Japikse, Enthea Press. An excellent short introduction to the ways we can work with angels.

*To Hear the Angels Sing: An Odyssey of Co-Creation with the Devic Kingdom*, Dorothy Maclean, Lindisfarne Press. One of the founders of Findhorne discusses her experiences with angels and how we can work with them to create.

The Kingdom of the Shining Ones, Natives of Eternity, and Rediscovering the Angels, Flower Newhouse, The Christward Ministry. Three volumes by the well-known mystic, who explores her own insights into the angelic kingdom and its purpose.

Angels & Mortals: Their Co-Creative Power, Maria Parisen, ed., Quest Books. A fascinating compilation of excerpts and articles from many sources, including Native American, candomblé, psychology, and the teachings of Swedenborg and Steiner.

The Ministry of Angels, Here and Beyond, Joy Snell, Citadel Press. Subtitled A Personal Account of What Lies Beyond Death, this book preceded the famous Embraced by the Light by Betty Eadie. An interesting personal witness.

Creating with the Angels, Messengers of Light, * and Guardians of Hope, * Terry Lynn Taylor, H. J. Kramer. Three volumes from one of the most inspired angel authors in America.

## Children's Books

The Angels: God's Messengers & Our Helpers, Lawrence Lovasik, Catholic Book Publishing Co. Bible-based stories.

Angels Get No Respect, Cecile Bauer, Magnificat Press. Humorous short stories.

The Angel Who Forgot, Elisa Bartone, Simon & Schuster. Lovely story of an angel and a boy in need of healing.

Ladder of Angels, Madeleine L'Engle. Bible stories with beautiful illustrations.

Angel of God, Piera Paltro, St. Paul Books. Darling book based on the "Angel of God" prayer.

The ABCs of Angels, Donna Gates, Ballantine. As much for adults as children, with small drawings and delightful sayings.

The Tiny Angel, Elizabeth Koda-Callan, Workman Publishing. The story of a girl in a Christmas pageant. Comes with its own angel necklace.

*The Book of Angels*, Terrie Tomko, St. Paul Books. Bible-based stories told in rhyme. Scripture reference section in back.

*Coloring Book About Angels*, Catholic Book Publishing Co. Bible-based, with texts in rhyme.

*Angel of God Coloring Book*, St. Paul Books. Pretty pictures to color for small children.

*The Angel and the Wild Animal*, Michael Foreman, Atheneum. Story of a little boy who is an angel at heart and a pretend wild animal.

*An Angel for Solomon Singer*, Cynthia Rylant, Orchard Books. A lonely man is befriended by an angel (the waiter at his café). Excellent writing.

*Angels on Roller Skates*, Maggie Harrison, Candlewick Press. The angels are mostly implied in this cute book about a British family.

*Angels, Prophets, Rabbis, and Kings*, José Patterson, Bedrick/Blackie. Stories from Jewish tradition with beautiful illustrations.

*The Angel and the Soldier Boy*, Peter Collington, Knopf. A beautiful wordless picture book that tells the story of a toy soldier and an angel doll and their adventures while their owner sleeps.

*Why Can't Grownups Believe in Angels?* Marsha Sinetar, Triumph Books. A wonderful book about a child who sees an angel. Adults will love it, too.

*Pink Stars and Angel Wings*, Susan Ekberg, Spiritseeker Publishing. A beautiful story about a girl who dreams her angels come to take her on a journey. Great artwork.

*The Alabama Angels*, Mary Barwick, Ballantine. The only book I know of with angels of color. God sends them to help out the poor people of Alabama by night.

# Art Books and Angel Quotes

*Angels: An Endangered Species*, Malcolm Godwin, Simon & Schuster. Arguably the most beautiful picture book about angels, although the text is not as accurate as it might be.

*Angels*, Caroline Johnson, Barnes & Noble. A small picture book with twenty-six full-color plates of interesting angels from great artists, plus data on the paintings.

*Angels*, Peter Lamborne Wilson, Pantheon Books. Eclipsed by the Godwin book, I like this equally as well, and the illustrations are more unusual and diverse.

*The Angel Tree*, Lynn Howard and Mary Jane Poole, Knopf. Gorgeous history and photos of the angel tree at the Metropolitan Museum of Art.

*Angels: A Book to Keep and Fifteen Postcards to Send*, Chronicle Books. A small book and set of postcards packaged together. Nicely done.

*A Host of Angels*, Gail Harvey, Gramercy Books. A pretty book of angel art with quotes from a wide variety of literature.

*Angels and Cupids*, Sylvia Lawrence, Rizzoli. A quality picture book with appropriate quotes.

*An Angel a Week*, Ballantine. Small book with angel quotes.

Books from major publishers are generally available from most bookstores. New Age books can usually be ordered through metaphysical stores. If you have trouble locating a particular book, write to author John Ronner at Mamre Press, 107-AK South Second Avenue, Murfreesboro, TN 37130. He has the only mail-order business specializing just in books about angels.

# Appendix
# Further Resources for AngelWatchers

One of the purposes of The AngelWatch™ Foundation is to provide a network for people and organizations involved with angels to communicate with each other. The following makes no attempt to be complete. In fact, by the time you read this, *AngelWatch™* journal will have undoubtedly added dozens more resources. But this should get you started.

Please keep in mind that occasionally, one or more of these resources may change or discontinue its services/resources, and that most of these listings are fairly small, with limited resources. Subscription prices can change, and policies can be altered. However, as of February 1994 these listings were current.

If you write for further information, be sure to enclose a business-size, self-addressed stamped envelope (SASE). If the listing requests a dollar or two to cover the costs of a catalog, please include it. Many people with angel-related businesses work with a small budget. Please keep in mind that Warner Books is not responsible for any of these listings, or for the products and services they offer.

# National Organizations

**The AngelWatch™ Foundation, Inc.**
P.O. Box 1397, Mountainside, NJ 07092
This is my own organization for all information about angels and their work in the world today. The foundation publishes *AngelWatch™*, the only magazine about angels in the world, which appears every two months. Subscriptions to the magazine are $16 in the United States, $20 U.S. in Canada, and $25 U.S. elsewhere (for airmail delivery). Send SASE for more information in the United States; send long envelope and one I.R.C. in Canada and elsewhere.

**Angel Collectors Club of America**
16342 West Fifty-fourth Street, Golden, CO 80403
A large club for collectors, with local chapters, round robins, a biannual convention, a newsletter, and roster. Dues $12.

**Angels of the World**
2232 McKinley Ave., St. Albans, WV 25177
AWI is a smaller general-interest club, not just for collectors of angels, with round robins, a convention (held in alternate years to the ACCA convention), club newsletter. Write for information.

**Tapestry**
P.O. Box 3032, Waquoit, MA 02536
K. Martin-Kuri's organization sponsors an annual conference on angels and other activities. Write for information.

**Be an Angel Day**
Angelic Alliance, P.O. Box 95, Upperco, MD 21155
Jane Howard sponsors the annual Be an Angel Day. Write or call 410-833-6912.

# Religious Groups

**Philangeli (Friends of the Angels)**
1115 East Euclid Street, Arlington Heights, IL 60004
Catholic prayer organization.

**Opus Sanctorum Angelorum**
Marian Center, 134 Golden Gate Avenue
San Francisco, CA 94102
Catholic prayer organization.

**First Church of the Angels**
P.O. Box 4713, Carmel, CA 93921
New church that focuses on angels and healing.

**Questhaven**
P.O. Box 20560, Escondido, CA 92029
Sponsors religious retreats and workshops emphasizing angels. Rev. Flower Newhouse organization.

**Angel Walk**
P.O. Box 1027, Riverton, WY 82501
Nondenominational, religious-metaphysical center.

# Mail-Order and/or Retail Stores

## West Coast

**Angel Productions**
2219 Desert Creek, Simi Valley, CA 93063
A wide variety, including tapes and music boxes. Write for information.

**The Angels Rainbow**
464 Court Avenue, Ventura, CA 93003
Mail-order angelic/prosperity products.

**Marilynn's Angels**
275 Celeste Drive, Riverside, CA 92507

Angels from weather vanes to night-lights, retail and oldest angel mail-order business. Send $1 for catalog of great angel things.

**Tara's Angels**
31781 Camino Capistrano
San Juan Capistrano, CA 92675
Retail store, discussion groups, too. Call 714-248-8822.

**Angel de las Flores**
318 North Santa Cruz Avenue, Los Gatos, CA 95030
Opened six years ago, this Angel may be the oldest retail store specializing in angels. Call 408-354-3375.

**Ark Angels**
116 Main Street, Tiburon, CA 94939
Retail shop and mail order. Send SASE for mail-order list. Call 415-435-9077.

**The Red Rose Collection**
P.O. Box 1859 Burlingame, CA 94011
Unusual angels (and other good things) by mail order. Call 1-800-451-LOVE.

**The Fool's Journey—Marie Haddad**
1900 Vallejo, #201, San Francisco, CA 94123
The best angel Ts, sweats—even baby rompers. Write for a catalog.

**Angel Blessings**
P.O. Box 28471, San Diego, CA 92198
Angel cards. Send SASE for more information.

**Angels by the Sea**
75 Mount Hermon Road #C, Scotts Valley, CA 95066
Retail store. Call 408-439-0696.

**Crystal Angel**
740 El Camino Real, Belmont, CA 94002
Retail store. Call 415-592-9539.

**Heaven on Earth**
1050 East Walnut Street, Pasadena, CA 91106
Retail store. Call 818-585-1569.

**Cheerful Cherub**
P.O. Box 26302, San Diego, CA 92196
Unusual catalog, many Catholic-style angels, unusual rubber stamps.

**Angel Star**
16190 Monterey Road, Morgan Hill, CA 95037
Angel-inspired stickers, cards, pins, signs; wholesale and retail. Write for catalog.

**A Gathering of Angels**
225 Main Street, Chico, CA
Retail store. Call 916-893-5055.

**Angels for Everyone**
27766 Berwick, Mission Viejo, CA 92691
Home business, shows.

**Wings 'n Things**
P.O. Box 873, Rancho Cucamonga, CA 91729
Mail-order catalog with angels. Call 909-945-5280.

**Wings**
226 North Mount Shasta Boulevard, Mount Shasta, CA 96067
Retail store. Call 916-926-3041.

**Caroline Sutherland**
P.O. Box 70, Hansville, WA 98340
Caroline's story of how she was touched by angels and given a gift of healing was told in *Touched by Angels*. She has developed a soft, cuddly angel doll and positive reinforcement tapes for children that are excellent. It's called "My Little Angel Tells Me I'm Special." Call 206-638-2607.

**Angels & Us**
3257 S.E. Hawthorne Boulevard, Portland, OR 97214
Retail store and permanent angel art gallery. Wonderful place! Peter and Karen Davis also have a large number of angel-related tapes and books for people who are visually impaired.

**All About Angels**
10767 Butte Street NE, Butteville, OR 97002
Retail store located inside old general store.

**Angel Communications, Inc.**
Suite 205—1089 West Broadway Avenue
Vancouver, BC V6H 1E5 Canada
Store, newsletter, seminars, and more. Call 604-73-ANGEL for information.

**Blue Angel Boutique**
P.O. Box 7073 STN D, Victoria, BC V9B 4Z2 Canada
Retail, wholesale, and mail order. Call 604-642-7720.

**Angels Only . . . and Friends**
20439 Douglas Crescent, Langley, BC Z3A 4B6 Canada
Retail store. Call 604-534-2244.

## East Coast

**Little Angels**
1275 Bloomfield Avenue, Building 1, Door 7
Fairfield, NJ 07004
Retail store, mail order, and wholesale business, Victorian and other angels with potpourri and fragrance. The owner, Tomoyo Rezvani, makes all her angels by hand. Call 201-808-6908 for a catalog.

**The Littlest Angel**
921 Landis Avenue, Vineland, NJ 08360
Retail store. Call 609-691-9588.

**Everything Angels**
P.O. Box 467, New York, NY 10028
1-800-99-ANGEL
A large mail-order catalog with great variety. Send $2 for catalog, refundable with order. Retail store, too; call for location.

**Dolores Devine**
P.O. Box 4323, Winter Park, FL 32793
Angel-inspired music tapes with prayer for healing. Send SASE for information. Great tapes.

**The St. Michael Shop**
20 Commerce Street, Flemington, NJ
Angel gifts, many books.

**Angels Express**
P.O. Box 8094, Gaithersburg, MD 20898
Angelic mail order. Call 301-216-2638.

**Heavenly Scents**
5827 Stony Hill Road, New Hope, PA 18938
Retail and wholesale cherubs and angels. Some very nice designs.

**Angel Fare**
84 Main Street, Torrington, CT 06790
New retail store.

**Angel Wings**
PO Box 430, Hope, NJ 07844
Special potpourri. Write for wholesale information.

**Necessary Angel**
37 Harvard, Brookline, MA 02146
Retail store. Call 617-277-2114.

**Angelica**
7 Central Street, Salem, MA 01970
Retail store. Call 508-745-9355.

**Angels Loft**
Route 18, North Bedford Street, East Bridgewater, MA 02333
Retail store. Call 808-378-8333.

**Cherubs**
1 Deerfield Avenue, Shelburne Falls, MA 01370
Retail store. Call 413-625-2545.

**Creative Gifts**
54 Horizon View Drive, Colchester, VT 05446
Country-style heirloom angels.

**Buffaloflowers**
1125 Summerwood Circle, Wellington, FL 33414
Soft-sculpture angels, kitchen angels, christening angels, country-style natural materials.

**Inner Spaces**
403 West Weaver Street, Carrboro, NC 27510
Retail store.

**Angelic Bookstore**
111 Central Avenue, Gaithersburg, MD 20876
Retail store. Call 301-840-0207.

**Heavens to Betsy**
Bankers Galleria, 8098 Main St., Ellicott City, MD 21043
Retail store.

**Heaven on Earth**
P.O. Box 40335, Washington, DC 20016
Beautiful children's angel dolls, soft and cuddly and sweet, in all the
colors of God's human rainbow, retail and wholesale. The owner gives
at least 10% of pre-tax profits to children's charities. Right now they're
helping build an orphanage in Bosnia. I think they're angels!
Call 1-800-351-ANGEL.

**Something Angelic Within**
1212½ W. Cary, Richmond, VA 23220
Jeff Camp has some really neat angel T's, plus rubber stamps! Write for
a catalog.

**Mamre Press**
107-AFS. Second Avenue, Murfreesboro, TN 37130
John Ronner has the largest catalog just of angel books anywhere, besides
being a well-known author himself. Send SASE for catalog.

**Christmas Country Angels**
Route 108, Plaistow, NH 03865
All sorts of angels. Write for catalog.

**Heavenly Hosts**
P.O. Box 86, Snellville, GA 30278
Beautiful handcrafted angels in ceramic, glass, fabric, etc. Send $1 for
catalog.

**Angel Kissed Chocolate**
P.O. Box 17561, Plantation, FL 33318
Heavenly confections. Write for a catalog.

**Angel Connection**
7332 Exter Way, Tampa, FL 33615
Ceramic angels by Rose Lenore. Call 813-884-9180.

**Among the Angels**
402 Laskin Road, Virginia Beach, VA 23451
Retail store.

**Angel Gallery & Gifts**
6224 Summer Pond Drive East, Centerville, VA 22020
Retail store. Call 703-815-8630.

**Hearts Desire**
103 Bronx Dr., Cheektowaga, NY 14227-3268
Gorgeous hand-painted angels on T's, sweats. Write for more information. Call 716-656-1220.

## Central/Mountain Regions

**The Angel Lady**
216 South Spring Street, Independence, MO 64050
Retail store. Call 816-252-5300.

**Angel Kisses of St. Charles**
504 East Main Street, Charles, IL 60174
Retail store with wide variety of angels.

**Angels for All Seasons**
3100 South Sheridan Boulevard, Denver, CO 80227
Retail store.

**Angels Are Light**
P.O. Box 470035, Aurora, CO 80047-0035
Angel gifts catalog with cards, stickers, angel confettios, and more, plus newsletter ($1.00 for catalog, refundable with order).

**Angel Station**
835 Main Avenue, Durango, CO 81301
Retail store. Call 303-382-0244.

**Angels & Things**
8236 East Seventy-first Street, Tulsa, OK 74133
Write to Penny Baker for more information.

**Angel Peace**
115 Northeast Timber Creek Road, Lee's Summit, MI 64064
Retail store.

**Special Signatures**
11334 Earlywood Drive, Dallas, TX 75218
Hand-painted cards, postcards, original books of angel poetry/legends.
Send SASE for more information.

**Tin Angel**
1402 Fifth Street, Seabrook, TX 77586
Retail store and tea room. Call 713-474-7978.

**Celestial Angels**
728 Arledge, Azle, TX 76020
Retail store. Call 817-444-5862.

**The Whistling Angel**
2420 Live Oak, San Angelo, TX 76901
Mail order: beautiful hand-crafted angels, stamps, etc.

**Everyday Angels**
5739 Lover's Lane, Shreveport, LA 71105
Retail store. Call 318-869-1947.

**Angels of the Sea**
40 Norman Ridge Drive, Bloomington, MN 55437
Ornaments and guardian angel plaques made of colorful seashells.

**Angel Treasures**
401 North Main, Royal Oak, MI 78067
Retail store. Call 810-548-5799.

**Angels Art & Crystals**
3006 West Highway 89A, Sedona, AZ 86339
Retail store. Call 602-282-7089.

# Jewelry

**Angel World**
P.O. Box 210425, Columbia, SC 29210

Martha Powers, whose story was told in *Touched by Angels*, invented the idea of wearing a guardian angel on one's shoulder. Her angel-inspired designs, in pewter, silver, and gold, are beautiful. Write for information.

**Hand and Hammer**
Woodbridge, VA
H & H makes the most elaborate sterling angels I know of, cast by the lost-wax process, for ornaments, or for wearing as pins or pendants. They have produced at least thirty or forty designs, all taken from great artworks. Call for catalog and newspaper, which shows pictures of all designs. Call 1-800-SILVERY.

**Jeff Stewart Antiques**
P.O. Box 105, Newton, SC 28658
Jeff has many silver angel ornaments/jewelry, including old H&H designs. Send $2 for catalog.

**James Avery Craftsman**
PO Box 1367, Kerrville, TX 78029
Silver/gold angel charms, earrings, bracelets, rings, etc. Beautiful quality. Catalog, retail stores. Call 1-800-283-1770.

# ARTISTS

**Lois East**
2097 South Devinney Street, Lakewood, CO 80228
Lois paints spiritual interpretations of people's angels in pastels.

**Andy Lakey**
40485-D Murrieta Hot Springs Road
Murrieta, CA 92563
Andy told his extraordinary story of how God led him to paint angels in *Touched by Angels*, where his first angel work, "My Seven Angels," graces the endpapers. He created a special angel painting for the endpapers of this book. Andy paints what he calls the spiritual essence of the angel who came to him in a near-death encounter, and his very abstract angels are full of spiritual power and energy. Andy often donates his angel

Eileen Elias Freeman

paintings to raise money for children, especially those with disabilities or AIDS. He welcomes inquiries from groups interested in his donation program. Andy's paintings are unique in that he often uses paint laid on in thick lines so even visually impaired persons can feel his works.

**Mariann Loveland**
444 North Aurora Street, Ithaca, NY 14850
Mariann is an exceptionally fine artist whose angels have been exhibited at many shows.

**Sandra Martindale**
P.O. Box 955, Black Mountain, NC 28711
Sandra paints the guardian angels of other people that she senses through prayer and meditation.

**K. Martin-Kuri**
Tapestry, P.O. Box 3032, Waquoit, MA 02536
The founder of Tapestry (see Organizations) is a gifted fine artist whose angel paintings reflect her own deeply spiritual outlook.

**Kathy Sellick Nadalin**
P.O. Box 921, Woodstock, NY 12498
A clairvoyant and artist, Kathy's angel paintings often include her own angel, Haniel.

**Louise Roach**
Pardus, Inc., 28 Moya Loop, Santa Fe, NM 87505
Louise works with new art media to create most unusual angel art. Send SASE for more information.

**Sally Simonetti**
OTW Productions, 1541 North Laurel Avenue, #105
Los Angeles, CA 90046
Sally's angel paintings and photographic prints depict powerful, elegant, spiritual beings.